*strive
for truth!*

PART THREE

מכתב מאליהו

RABBI ELIYAHU E. DESSLER

strive for truth!

MICHTAV ME-ELIYAHU

the selected writings of Rabbi E.E. Dessler

rendered into English and annotated by

Aryeh Carmell

FELDHEIM PUBLISHERS

Jerusalem □ New York

Strive for Truth!

PART THREE

First Published 1989
Hardcover edition: 0-87306-519-0
Paperback edition: 0-87306-520-4

Published by permission
of the Committee for Publication
of the Writings
of Rabbi E. E. Dessler

Feldheim Publishers Ltd.
POB 6525/Jerusalem, Israel

Philipp Feldheim Inc.
200 Airport Executive Park
Spring Valley, NY 10977

Printed in Israel

contents

WORLDS

preface

This third volume of *Strive for Truth!* completes the English version of *Michtav Me-Eliyahu* Volume I, a book which, together with its companion volumes, has influenced the thinking of a whole generation.

As mentioned in the Preface to the second volume of *Strive for Truth!*, the contents of *Michtav Me-Eliyahu* Volume I were arranged in order of increasing difficulty. It follows that many of the articles and essays in the present volume will be found more "difficult" than their predecessors. In particular, concepts from the world of *kabbala* make frequent appearance. Here Rabbi Dessler shows fascinating correspondences between these seemingly recondite matters and the spiritual realities of our inner life. Using profound insights from both *mussar* and *kabbala*, Rabbi Dessler proceeds to illuminate, among other things, the mysteries of atonement, the philosophic problem of determinism and free will, and the meaning of religious language. Towards the end of the book Rabbi Dessler makes a breathtaking attempt — unique, I think, in all our literature — to lift the veil on the pulsating rhythms of life in the World to Come. This occurs in the series entitled "Being and Having."

All in all, the industrious reader will find himself (or herself) immensely stimulated and enriched, both intellectually and spiritually, by this amazing book.

I am grateful to Hashem for having brought me thus far along the road, and I pray that He may grant life and strength to enable me to continue and complete this great endeavor.

Jerusalem, Tammuz 5748   ARYEH CARMELL

The Voice of Eliyahu

□□

From a letter sent by Rabbi Dessler from England to Ponevezh Yeshiva, Bnei Brak, in Nissan 5708 (April 1948). It was clear that historical events were in the making. Was the final act of the world drama at hand?

The voice of Eliyahu

□□□□□□□□□□□□□□□□□□□□□□□□□□□□□□□□□□□□□□□

To appreciate the events of our time, we need concentration and careful observation, and these, in turn, need a tranquil mind. Then we shall see these events quite differently from the way others see them; we shall evaluate them differently and act differently as a consequence.

Intellectually speaking, we know a good deal about the era of *'ikvata demashiḥa* (the footsteps of *Mashiaḥ*). But this does not seem to involve us in drawing any practical conclusions. It has always been like that. Some people see what's going on; some are dimly aware but do not *see*. And there are others for whom the events have not yet reached even the threshold of their awareness. [The Midrash[1] tells us that when Avraham saw in the distance the mountain on which the *akeyda* was to be carried out:

> He said to Yitzḥak: Do you see anything? He replied: Yes, I see a mountain with a cloud attached to it. Avraham then turned to the servants and asked: Do you see anything? They answered: No. Whereupon he said to them, "You stay here with the donkey,"[2] i.e., Just as the donkey sees but knows not what it sees, so

do you. [In this respect, there are people who resemble donkeys.]

"There are people who resemble donkeys" — just because they do not see what they ought to see. If the earlier generations were like humans, then we are like donkeys, say the Rabbis.[3] Like donkeys... plodding... animal-like... interested only in material things. If this is what our Sages called *themselves*, then what is left for us to be compared to?

Yes, we are indeed a very long way from seeing things properly and hearing them accurately. But still, what Heaven shows us is meant to be seen. We must not deceive ourselves by saying we *cannot* see. If we look carefully we shall find that our eyes are opened.

Our Rabbis in the Midrash, on the verse, "The voice of my beloved — here he comes," have recorded the following amazing prediction:[4]

> When the sound of the [Messianic] *shofar* is heard, twenty disasters come into the world; in ten places people are killed, in ten places people are burnt (*"ten" signifies a community; the reference is to a general decree of slaughter, a general decree of burning. To our sorrow we have had no lack of furnaces, no lack of weapons in the hands of the murderers.*) This teaches us that the door (*of inner redemption*) is not opened all at once; but Eliyahu...comes to one city and is hidden from another, speaks to one person and is hidden from another.

On the subject of communications from Eliyahu, Maharal of Prague tells us in a similar vein, "On many occasions Eliyahu may communicate certain matters to a person without that person knowing their true origin. They seem to him to be his own thoughts, but in fact they are communications from Eliyahu."[5]

How can we possibly not be aware of what is going on around us? Has the *shofar* not been sounding strongly enough throughout the whole world for decades now? Have there not been unceasing war-sirens and disasters threatening to demolish the very fabric of the world? What about Communism? What about the incurable ills of the world economy? And then: universal decrees of killing and burning, directed against *us*. And we still cannot hear inside our minds what Eliyahu is trying to tell us?

Until we attune our ears to his words and observe what he is trying to show us, there can be no repentance and no chance to merit the coming of *Mashiaḥ*. Our Rabbis have made this quite clear in the following passage:[6]

> Rabbi Yehuda says, if the people of Yisrael do not repent they will not be redeemed. And they will not repent unless they suffer the pains of instability and lack of livelihood (*the siege of Jerusalem etc.*[7]), and they will not repent until Eliyahu comes, as it says, "Behold I am sending you Eliyahu the prophet before the coming of the great and terrible day of Hashem, and he will restore the hearts of the fathers to the children, etc."

We have already seen above that the coming of Eliyahu can be a very individual matter. It follows that final repentance can come only to that individual who hears the voice of Eliyahu speaking to *him*. And what of the one who does not want to hear? He will not repent and will not merit redemption.

Are we never going to realize that the final hour is

approaching? Are we still going to play with our child-
ish toys and insist on embracing the idols of a petty,
worthless paganism until it is too late? We all know of
people who remained devoted to their idols and hugged
and kissed them until their last breath.[8]

We can hardly fail to see the ironic vengeance of the
Other Side.[9] We had just been shown the "kindness" of
the nations.[10] (This was a historic testing time for us. If
we had the merit to raise our hearts at that moment in
sincerity to our Father in heaven, the nations would
perforce have kept their promise, as the Torah says,
"See I have set the land before you,"[11] and Rashi
comments, "There is no one to object and you will not
need to fight." If they had not descended to the level of
"nature" by sending the spies, they would never have
needed weapons to conquer Eretz Yisrael.)[12] In any
event, we made the mistake of trusting *them*, although
one of the conditions for repentance is to know that
"Ashur shall not save us."[13] And what happened? All
the nations assembled to make decrees against us,
something that has never happened before.[14] (Who can
deliver us into the hands of murderers if Hashem does
not abandon us?)

If we think there is plenty of time, we may well be
mistaken. All that has been foretold for the era of the
birth pangs of *Mashiah* has been fulfilled. "A king as
bad as Haman,"[15] decrees, burnings and slaughter,
famine and deprivation — all has come true before our
eyes. "The spread of the evil kingdom"[16] has come
true, and all the nations are gathering against us. Is
there any time left? Can we still delay listening to the
message of Eliyahu? There is no better month than
Nissan, the month of redemption, to merit hearing the

sound of the great *shofar* and the voice of Eliyahu, as
our Rabbis say, "In Nissan we were once redeemed and
in Nissan shall be our future redemption."[17] If not
now, when?

□□□□□□□

We must strengthen ourselves with every fiber of our
being, and then we shall be able to withstand all on-
slaughts. If our resolve is nothing but lip service, full of
enthusiasm today, but gone tomorrow, then we have
neither seen nor heard *anything*. Such resolves are
worthless. If we make our group a sincere Torah community, all well and good. If not, what is the good of
pretending? What is the point of a Torah community
engaged in playing games? If slackness is the rule, we
have gained nothing, we have achieved nothing. Have
we not spent enough years in self-deception? It is absolutely essential that we put a stop once and for all to
publicly organized self-deception.

We must strengthen ourselves in Torah learning
with intensive effort and true persistence. We must
resolve to devote ourselves daily to *mussar* learning and
reflection *with the truth perspective*.[18] Only then will we
begin to perceive in our hearts true insights we had not
previously perceived, and truths we had never previously realized. Through spiritual effort we shall
merit heavenly aid and through "truth perspective" we
shall merit redemption.   □

notes

1 *Bereshit Rabba* 56:2.
2 *Bereshit* 22:5.

3 *Shabbat* 112b.

4 *Yalkut Shimoni* on *Shir Ha-shirim* 2:8.

5 *Netzaḥ Yisrael*, ch. 28.

6 *Yalkut Shimoni, Malachi*, end.

7 The reference is to the events of 1947-48.

8 See *Sanhedrin* 64a.

9 The power of evil implanted in the universe by God as a test for our free will. It is called by the kabbalists *sitra aḥara* (the other side) or the "rear" of the structure of holiness in the universe.

10 This refers to the United Nations vote of November 29, 1947, agreeing to the formation of a Jewish State in part of Palestine.

11 *Devarim* 1:8.

12 See Volume II, p. 263.

13 *Hoshea'* 14:4.

14 This may refer to the invasion of Eretz Yisrael by seven Arab armies with the tacit acquiescence of the United Nations.

15 *Sanhedrin* 97b.

16 Ibid. 98b.

17 *Rosh Hashana* 11a.

18 See Volume I, p. 160 et seq.

Torah and Mitzvot

☐☐☐☐☐☐☐☐☐☐☐☐☐☐☐☐☐☐☐☐☐☐☐☐☐☐☐☐☐☐☐☐☐☐☐☐☐☐☐

The first two essays in this series, written in the last year of Rabbi Dessler's life, present with great force and clarity one of the basic themes of his teaching — the centrality of Torah study in the spiritual life of the Jews.

They are also distinguished by several examples of Rabbi Dessler's unique ability to translate kabbalistic concepts into psycho-ethical (*mussar*) realities.

Mental attachment to Torah

PART ONE

□□

My saintly great-grandfather, Rabbi Yisrael Salanter, wrote in his famous *Mussar Letter*[1] as follows:

> The most sublime and most essential of the Torah's therapeutic methods for the cure of *yetzer*-induced [spiritual] diseases is to study with intensity and at great depth the laws connected with the particular sin [to which one is prone]...This is a powerful tool and may succeed gradually in endowing the psyche with important values...But there is another aspect of a spiritual nature, *whose causes remain unrecognized by the human intellect and senses*, and which is referred to by our Rabbis when they say "Torah saves one [from sin] at the time one is occupied with it."[2] And it saves him from sin no matter which part of the Torah he is occupied with. He may study the case of "the ox which gores the cow" (*Bava Kamma*, ch. 5) or similar matters, and it will save him from [the completely unrelated sin of] evil speech...*for the spirituality of Torah preserves him.*[3]

We must consider this carefully. The Torah says, "You shall know today, and return it to your heart [that Hashem is God in heaven above and on the earth below...]"[4] "You shall know" refers to intellectual knowledge; "return it to your heart" means knowledge which penetrates into the subconscious and so influences our actions.] There is a vast empty space in the human psyche, situated between intellectual knowledge and its realization in the heart. Only when he achieves a close association of "knowledge" and "heart," with no gulf in between, will a person's actions accord with his knowledge. As soon as there is a gap between these two, the *yetzer ha-ra'* entrenches itself in the resulting vacuum and entry is given to all the yearnings and imaginings of this world. All the thoughts emanating from man's selfish nature have their place there, and from there they proceed to conquer the heart. "The eye sees and the heart desires."[5] "The eye sees" by entering into the empty space; the immediate consequence is "the heart desires." This is what arouses Rabbi Yisrael's astonishment elsewhere in the *Mussar Letter*,[6] when he notes that "Man is free in his imagination but fettered by his intellect." The imaginings of the world develop by themselves with the utmost ease from mere knowledge to heart's desire. But when it comes to matters of the mind, how long is the way from "and you shall know" to "and return it to your heart"!

CONQUERING INNER SPACE

This space between "knowledge" and "heart," then, is the arena of the war with the *yetzer* — the place where free will is exercised. It follows that our first goal must be to capture this space. If we succeed in this, good prospects open up for all our moral decisions.

How can we set about conquering this space? Rambam counsels us that the most powerful method of preventing lustful thoughts is "to broaden one's mind with wisdom, for lustful thoughts flourish only in a mind devoid of wisdom."[7] This means that if one loves "wisdom" (that is, intellectual pursuits), and allows it to dominate his mind — even if the subject matter has nothing to do with the avoidance of lust — this will prevent the emergence of evil thoughts altogether. If all that vast domain of empty mental space is filled with wisdom, if his interest and emotional attachment are directed single-mindedly to that end, then there will no longer be any room for lustful thoughts to enter. He will have no eyes, no ears, no thoughts for anything but the wisdom he loves, and so he will be saved from the entry of lust into his heart.

If this is true of any wisdom, any intellectual pursuit that captures one's interest, how much more is it true if the wisdom which engages his interest is that of the Divine Torah. Then there is a very powerful additional force in operation. The sanctity of the Torah will pervade his being and its spirituality will preserve him from defilement.

Furthermore, as we know, there is an indestructible "holy point" within every Jewish heart, conforming to the mystical meaning of the verse "I have never rejected them...to utterly destroy them."[8] And "a little light casts out much darkness,"[9] so that if the empty space is cleared of the *yetzer ha-ra‘* to even a small extent, this will allow the "holy point" to expand into the space, and his inner life will begin to influence his outer life.

TORAH PROTECTS MITZVOT

This will enable us to understand the words of the Zohar,[10] "Rabbi Elazar commenced his discourse with the verse, 'And I placed My word in your mouth and

with the shadow of My hands I have covered you.'¹¹
[This means] that the Holy One blessed be He covered
him and the Shechina spread its wings over him.'"⁹
Rabbi Isaac Ḥaver, a disciple of the Vilna Gaon,
explains that "placing my word in your mouth" refers
to Torah study. If a person loves to study Torah and to
pursue its knowledge, he will succeed in banishing the
yetzer ha-ra' from his heart.¹⁰

This explains why one always speaks of "Torah and
mitzvot." Why is Torah study not included among the
mitzvot? The reason is that Torah protects the observance of all the mitzvot. This is the meaning of the
well-known saying, "If it were not for My covenant day
and night [if it were not for constant Torah study], I
never would have established the laws of heaven and
earth."¹² If it were not for the sanctification made
possible by attachment to Torah study, the whole creation would not have been feasible. It would be very
improbable that people would keep mitzvot if sanctity
were not preserved in the *beḥira*-space by attachment
to Torah learning. [And without mitzvot there would
be no point in creation.]

Another wonderful idea on this topic is cited by R.
David ibn Zimra (Radbaz):¹³

> You should know that each yeshiva here below is paral-
> leled by a yeshiva on high, consisting of the souls of the
> *tsaddikim* who studied Torah in this world. Those who
> have their bodily existence below are paralleled by
> protective powers above, and all of them have their
> being in *Knesset Yisrael*. When they labor in Torah in
> this world, the corresponding forces labor in Torah
> above, and as a result the channels are straightened out
> and the world persists. — From *Sefer Ha-kaneh*

We can understand this as follows. In each member of Klal Yisrael there is a fine point of holiness. Being a point of inwardness, it combines with the inwardness of all Israel in all generations — that is, with all that has been revealed of God's glory by all the great and holy *tsaddikim* of the past, including the Patriarchs, Mosheh Rabbenu, etc.[14]

But only the inward point, which is spiritual, can effect this combination, not actions done by rote, without the inward motivation. The special nature of Torah learning, however, ensures that even its "outwardness" is "inward." Even if one learns for motives other than pure attachment to Hashem, the Giver of the Torah, if one learns because of one's attachment to Torah itself, simply out of love of Torah, this also counts as inwardness. Love of Torah is, after all, spiritual love, and this, too, is considered an aspect of *lishmah* (as discussed by the Gaon of Vilna and R. Ḥayyim of Volozhyn).[15] How wonderful to think that *every member of a yeshiva*, even in our orphaned generation, is united with the yeshivot of Beit Shammai and Beit Hillel and all the great ones of the past by virtue of his participation (at least) in the revelation of love of Torah. That is what is hinted at by saying that he has "protective powers above." We know that the meaning of "above," relative to ourselves, refers to the points of inwardness within us.[16]

One result of our labor in Torah cited by Radbaz was that "the channels are straightened." God's input into the world is said to be by way of crooked channels when the lessons must be conveyed through suffering and exile. But if the world is worthy, it receives an influx of good things which will be used as tools for the service of Hashem. This occurs when spiritual inwardness is strong, as it says, "If you will listen...I will give the rain of your land in its due season, etc." [This is called input by way of straight channels, for this is how things were meant to be.]

We learn from this that the influx of good things to Klal Yisrael in this world depends entirely on those who learn Torah with devotion and commitment.

A final quotation from Radbaz:

> ...Our Rabbis said that every word that issues from the mouth of God results in the creation of an angel, as it says, "And all their host by the breath of His mouth." If the word is merciful, angels of mercy are created, and if the opposite, the opposite. Similarly, when man, created in the image of God, studies Torah, an angel is created to speak for him and defend him, and this is the meaning of the saying, "Torah learning is equal to them all"[17] [i.e., to all the mitzvot].

We know that the concept of "angel" means a mission of positive teachings. An "accusing angel" means a mission whose purpose is to seduce man. "Seduction" and "accusation" are essentially one and the same, according to Rav Nissim and the author of *Tseda La-derech*.[18] It follows that an angel bearing heavenly aid and spiritual protection is called a "defending angel." This is equivalent to what was said in the Zohar — that devotion to Torah study gives special protection from Hashem.

Throwing oneself completely into Torah learning prevents all the accusations and seductions, and this is the reason it is greater than any mitzva. □

Mental attachment to Torah

PART TWO

□□

We say in the blessing over the Torah, "who has given us a Torah of truth and [thereby] planted everlasting life in our midst." The Torah of truth brings about the growth of spiritual life. This seems to be a special attribute of Torah study; we do not find this in connection with other mitzvot. Why should this be so?

Thought has its limits. We cannot think about anything of which we have no conception. We think by means of words and ideas which represent concepts known to us. For example, a person who has never had the sense of smell will not be able to think about smells. They are not within his conceptual range. We could perhaps give him some idea of what smell means by comparing it with other senses that are familiar to him. We could say that smell is to the nose what taste is to the palate. This would give him some idea. We could add that just as the ear picks up sound waves in the air, so the nose perceives something else in the air, and this is what is called smell. Even with this additional information, he will never be able to think about smell as it really is. Putting two and two together, he will be able to conclude that smell is something in the air, it is "tasty," and it is perceived by the nose. You may ask, since taste and hearing are so different from each other, how can smell resemble both? The answer is obvious: Smell, too, is different from both, but it still makes sense to compare them since there is one aspect in which it resembles each of them.

WHAT IS GEHINNOM?

Many difficult questions are answered by this analogy. For example, in the case of Gehinnom we have been given several apparently conflicting explanations. We have been told that it is (a) a terrible fire, (b) spiritual pain and remorse, (c) nonexistence. (These concepts are explained at length elsewhere in this volume.)[1] The reconciliation of these conflicting descriptions lies in the fact that we have no concept of spiritual pain in itself. We always have to relate it to something which mind and body have in common, otherwise our thoughts cannot lay hold of it at all. We have to grasp it by means of analogies. We must understand that the mental pain which is Gehinnom is certainly not less than the pain that would be caused by a fire sixty times hotter than ordinary fire.

The personality which survives death, after undergoing the purifying process of Gehinnom and other post-mortal processes, will eventually be freed from all mental attachment to worldly concerns. It will realize then that the idea of "good and evil" — when "evil" is considered a reality — is merely an illusion; truth is the only reality and falsehood is simply that which does not exist. It will then be possible to think about this world only by memories or by analogy.

This is how the righteous will "see the difference between the righteous and the wicked in the next world."[2] From the punishment of the wicked they will learn the justice and precision of God's judgment in all the subtle gradations of motive and responsibility and so on. All these things will find their ultimate justification by contributing in this way to the revelation of God's glory.

WISDOM'S VENGEANCE

Conversely, one who experienced no attachment to Torah in his lifetime will not be able to think about Torah in his post-mortal existence. My revered teacher, Rabbi Tzvi Broide, had wonderful things to say on this following passage in *Mishle*:[3]

> Wisdom shouts in the market
> She gives forth her voice in the streets
> How long will you thoughtless people love
> thoughtlessness
> And fools hate knowledge?...
> Because you refused when I called
> And when I stretched out my hand no one
> listened...
> I too will smile at your calamity
> I will mock when your terror comes.
> When your terror comes like a whirlwind...
> *Then they will call me and I will not answer,*
> *They will seek me and not find me.*

The calamity referred to is the death of the body. One who failed to make the wisdom of the Torah part of himself while he had the chance will not be able to direct his thought to it after his death. It is an act of grace that we are able to grasp Torah thoughts during our lifetime, even though our inner essence is not united with Torah. After death this no longer applies. We shall grasp in our thought only that which has become a reality in our inner self. "I shall mock when your terror comes...Then they will call me and I will not answer..." Such is the vengeance of the Torah on those who desecrated her honor! "Happy is he who comes here [to the next world] with his Torah learning in his hand"[4] — that is, the Torah which has become one with his own self. We are told that the Torah a person has acquired *is* his "World to Come."

Now we can understand the passage we referred to at the beginning of this article, "He gave us a Torah of truth and thereby planted everlasting life in our midst." Only the acquisition of Torah during our lifetime leads to the growth of everlasting spiritual life.[5]   □

notes (part one)

1 *Iggeret Ha-mussar*, first published in Koenigsberg, 1858. Subsequently published in standard editions of *Or Yisrael*, p. 103 et seq.
2 *Sota* 21b.
3 *Or Yisrael*, p. 106.
4 *Devarim* 4:39.
5 *Bamidbar Rabba* 10:12.
6 In the opening words of the poetic introduction.
7 *Mishneh Torah*, "Laws of Forbidden Unions," end.
8 *Vayikra* 26:44. See below.
9 R. Menaḥem b. Zeraḥ (14th c. Spain) in *Tseda La-derech*, no. 12.
10 Zohar III, 35a, based on *Yesha'ya* 51:16.
11 *Yesha'ya* 51:16.

12 In his commentary on the Vilna Gaon's *Ma'alot Ha-Torah*, no. 101.

13 *Metzudat David, Mitzvat Talmud Torah* (mitzva 22). Radbaz lived in Egypt in the sixteenth century.

14 It has already been explained, at the end of "Why the Righteous Suffer" (Volume I, p. 89), that all forms of spiritual endeavor are basically *kiddush Hashem*, that is, revealing God's glory and honoring, sanctifying and exalting His holy name throughout the universe. — A.C.

15 See *Ruah Hayyim*, ch. 6.

16 Presumably, "powers" refers to the spiritual powers released by our Torah study. "Shade" refers to the protection granted us.

17 *Mishna, Pe'ah* 1:2.

18 See note 9 above.

notes (part two)

1 See pp. 206 et seq.

2 *Malachi* 3:18.

3 *Mishle* 1:20-28.

4 *Pesahim* 50a.

5 See "Being and Having," pp. 185 et seq.

□□

This *shiur* was given in Ponevezh, Bnei Brak, *Parashat Naso* 5713 and in Gateshead the following week.

Torah: inward and outward

THE RELATIONSHIP BETWEEN INTELLECTUAL RESEARCH AND SPIRITUAL COMMITMENT

□□□□□□□□□□□□□□□□□□□□□□□□□□□□□□□□□□□□□□□

We wrote in the "Discourse on Free Will," Part II:[1]

> When we look into our own minds we observe firstly
> "selfhood" — our own ego...We also have senses by
> which the ego becomes aware of that which is outside
> itself...Our senses can perceive only the externals of
> objects, never their true essence..."Inner perception"
> — awareness of self — is not mediated by any of the
> senses...It is internal, intuitive knowledge of the most
> intimate kind.

Other items discerned by our inner consciousness
include our feelings and perceptions, and the point of
"attachment" of ego to body (our sense of being alive).
With these we can include basic moral values, such as
honesty, love, gratitude and so on. All these are given
without need of intellectual justification. Indeed, their
essence cannot be grasped by any rational argument;
they cannot even be conceptualized. They are all
grasped only by the inner self; they are what we call
inner intuitions.[1]

On the other hand, there are those things which can
be perceived by the senses, in their outward form, if not
in their essence. Here rational thought holds full sway;

the "how" and the "why" are legitimate objects of
scrutiny.

TWO APPROACHES

We find the same two approaches in Torah:

(1) A person can absorb the inner essence of Torah
according to the degree of purity he possesses. In the
Torah there are *ḥukkim* and *mishpatim. Ḥukkim*,
whose reasons are not given, are grasped by such a
person in their inner value. His closeness to Hashem —
his *devekut* — precludes any need to probe them with
his intellect. He does not need to know *why* his Creator wanted them; it is enough for him that He *did* want
them. *Mishpatim*, which human reason would require
even if they had not been commanded, can be grasped
by the intellect. But the person who is close to God is
so aware of his own unimportance that it does not enter
his mind to observe the mitzvot for any reason other
than that they are the will of the Almighty. His closeness to Hashem is his all-absorbing interest, and he is
guided neither by need nor expediency; all is of no
account except his closeness to Hashem.

(2) One who has not yet reached closeness to
Hashem will use his intellect to reinforce his duty to
observe the *mishpatim*. He will observe *ḥukkim* too,
out of a sense of obligation. This is the level of *yir'at
Hashem*. It is of great value, but it is not *devekut*. The
level of *yir'a* in relation to *devekut* can be compared to
the level of the child who is learning the *aleph-bet* in
relation to the adult who is learning Gemara. The child
sits on the adult's lap and sees his familiar *aleph-bet* in
the page of the Gemara. What he sees is true, but it is

very far from the whole truth. The adult is hardly aware of the letters, or of their combination into words; he is absorbed in the *ideas* behind the words. This is something the child can have no inkling of. Similarly, all intellectual achievements fade into nothingness compared with the inner truth of *devekut*.

We must probe further the relationship between intellectual inquiry and spiritual commitment, or *devekut*.

(1) Intellectual inquiry has two aspects: "how" and "why." In Torah this means "How is the mitzva to be performed?" — the details of the mitzva; and "Why is it to be performed?" — the reason for the mitzva.

(2) The question about the details of the mitzva is legitimate at all levels. Even Mosheh Rabbenu, on his supreme level of *devekut*, learned the details of mitzvot, though they were revealed to him by prophecy, through his *devekut*, and not by rational deduction.

(3) "Why?" on the other hand is a very important question at all levels — except that of *devekut*. When a person expends intellectual effort and discovers the wondrous ideas underlying the mitzvot of the Torah, he may develop a love of Torah and an all-consuming interest in it. From attachment to Torah, he may come to love of the Giver of the Torah. When the Rabbis said that the Torah is a "cure for the *yetzer ha-ra'*," this may be what they had in mind — interest in Torah can bring one to love of God.

(4) But when one arrives at the level of *devekut* and complete subservience to Hashem, one begins to feel that the question "Why?" appears as if *I* propose to probe with my intellect the reasons behind His will, and to determine why *I* should "agree" with Him.

There is some slight hint here that my agreement carries some weight, which is in opposition to complete self-effacement.

(5) The peak of *devekut* therefore sees the disappearance of the question "Why?" in relation to the will of Hashem. At this level one no longer feels the element of "compulsion" in relation to *ḥukkim*. The *ḥok* becomes as transparently clear as the *mishpat*. Reasons are no longer relevant in a situation of *devekut*.

We find that Shlomo Ha-melech understood the whole Torah except the *ḥok* of the Red Heifer, while Mosheh Rabbenu understood this too.[2] The Rabbis are not speaking of intellectual understanding, but spiritual apprehension, "the seeing of the heart." Shlomo Ha-melech had resolved in his heart every *ḥok* of the Torah, except for the one which is apparently so irrational that in his heart he still felt to some extent "at a distance" from it. But for Mosheh Rabbenu, even this obstacle did not exist.

WHAT CANNOT BE TAUGHT

These two approaches to Torah involve important differences in regard to both teaching and learning:

Direct teaching can apply only in the intellectual mode. The insights of the heart cannot be taught. It is doubtful whether people can communicate at all at the level of the inner self. (Maybe this is what the wife of Rabbi Shim'on ben Ḥalafta meant when she asked, "Can people 'see' each other in the World to Come?")[3]

The inner truths of Torah are secrets which are incommunicable, just as the Rabbis say the mystical parts of Torah may be transmitted "only to one who is wise and understands by himself."[4] Mystical insights are not intellectual and they cannot be communicated via the intellect. One can talk about them only in a roundabout way so that the person who is ready for them can think around them until he eventually finds them in his own self. When the Rabbis said, "That which comes from the heart enters the heart [of another],"[5] they meant this indirect method of communication.

In the same way, by the exercise of *mussar* techniques, one can communicate ideas to one's own heart. [Anticipating Rabbi Yisrael Salanter by about six centuries] Rabbenu Yona Girondi, in his *Sha'arei Teshuva*,[6] set out the progress of *mussar* learning as follows:

> When hearing *mussar* [words of spiritual discipline] a person should (1) awaken his soul, (2) take the words to heart, (3) think of them *continually*, (4) add to them lessons of his own, (5) produce words from his heart, (6) isolate himself in the chambers of his spirit, (7) turn his rebuke upon himself, (8) his rebuke continuing morning by morning and minute by minute, until (9) his soul accepts the *mussar* and [*even more*] until (10) it becomes pure.

This is the way ideas can be made to penetrate the heart. In no circumstance will they do this by themselves.[7]

COMPLETE SINCERITY

The teacher, too, must restrain his eloquence when speaking of his own spiritual insights. When one is in touch with his inner self, he must be alone with his thoughts. When he needs to communicate, this must be done as an act of service. To attach oneself to God means to attach oneself to His attributes — "just as He is merciful, so are you merciful, etc."[8] The most profound aspect of *hesed* is when the kindness is done, not only for the sake of the other person, but also as an expression of attachment to Hashem and His supreme *hesed*. Then we may be sure it is completely sincere.

Rabbi Naftali Amsterdam [a leading disciple of Rabbi Yisrael Salanter] quoted the *Hatam Sofer* as saying that Avraham Avinu received special *hesed* from God to ensure that he did not lose his high spiritual perfection as a result of his constant contact with ordinary people on whom he bestowed acts of kindness. This is why God is referred to as "the shield of Avraham."

All attachment to matters outside oneself tends to diminish one's inwardness. Even worldly worries can be lessened by relating them to others.[9] Rabbi Simha Zissel refrained from telling others about those *mussar* insights which still had the power to affect his own heart. He knew that telling them to others releases the pressure, so to speak, and thus diminishes the effect on oneself. He is said to have kept one such insight to himself for twenty-five years for this reason.

This may be another reason why no attempt should be made to communicate mystical truths to others directly; the very act of expressing them would dim their effect on the speaker's mind. Once dimmed, the insight could never be restored. We are told that a penitent cannot reenter Torah life by the same way that he left it. (This is why the letter *hey* has a small aperture on the left "for the reentry of penitents.")[10] A spiritual light once dimmed cannot be reused; one must find a new way of arousing the heart.

So far we have been speaking of teaching. With regard to learning, the same two approaches apply. Originally, Torah was intended to be absorbed by inward insight; and so it would have been if not for the sins of Adam and the Golden Calf. But this is how Torah is absorbed in the spiritual world — *'Olam ha-ba*. We have already mentioned in the previous article that the intellectual mode of Torah learning is meant only for this world. In the next, we retain only that part of Torah which has been absorbed by our inner essence. "Happy is he who comes here with his learning in his hand"[11] — that is, the Torah which is part of his own personality *is* his *'Olam ha-ba*. When the Midrash speaks of Avraham Avinu learning Torah from two "sources of wisdom" which opened up in his own body,[12] they mean this mode of absorption from his own inner essence.

THE TWO TABLETS OF STONE

But the intellectual mode is important as a preparation for this, as we shall see.

We find these two modes reflected in the differences between the First Tablets (*Shemot* 31:18; 32:15-16) and the Second Tablets (*Shemot* 34:1). We have explained elsewhere[13] that the two sets of tablets correspond to the differing spiritual levels of Israel. Before they sinned, they were to receive tablets "from above" with the words "engraved on the stone," corresponding to their level of inwardness. Afterwards they received tablets prepared by Mosheh, and "written on" by God, corresponding to a lower level, wherein the ideas of the mind must be laboriously imprinted upon the heart.

That which is given "from above" must be earned by passing a test. This was the test presented by Mosheh's apparent delay. If the Israelites had passed this test, they would have "earned" the level given from above, and the Torah would have been "engraved upon their hearts," never to be forgotten. Since they did not, they henceforth had to operate on the lower level, by way of the intellect to reach the heart.

Maybe this is what is meant by the statement in *Tikkunei Zohar*[14] which compares the first Tablets to the level of the Tree of Life (i.e. inwardness), and the second to the level of the Tree of Knowledge of Good and Evil (i.e. working within the darkness and obscurity). Mosheh Rabbenu, of course, also received the Second Tablets by the inward mode; and his achievement was that he brought the Torah down for others into the world of knowledge of good and evil. Maybe this is what the Rabbis meant when they said that the Torah was originally given to Mosheh, and he was generous enough to give it to all of Israel.[15]

MOSHEH AND RABBI AKIVA

The Rabbis tell us that Mosheh asked God to allow him into the *beit ha-midrash* of Rabbi Akiva [about 1500 years ahead in time]. When he heard the *shiur*, he failed to understand it and was disturbed. His peace of mind was restored when he heard Rabbi Akiva refer to a certain law as *halacha l'Mosheh mi-Sinai*.[16] The meaning is that since Mosheh absorbed the whole Torah by the inward process, he tended to look down on the intellectual derivations perfected by Rabbi Akiva, which, in a sense, were tainted by outwardness. His mind was set to rest when he realized that through the intellect they, too, eventually arrived at the inner truth (*halacha l'Mosheh mi-Sinai*).

We read in the mystical classic *Pirkey Heychalot* (chapter 27) that the Jews did not want to build the Second Temple until they were assured by God that He would reveal to them the secrets of the Torah. The meaning is that, knowing that the era of prophecy was drawing to a close, they were concerned that they would be left with nothing but the outward approach to Torah. If this would be the case, they felt it would be inappropriate to build a Temple. God promised them, however, that through their intellectual endeavors in Torah they would eventually possess it in the depths of their hearts.

This is a great consolation to us today. Living as we do in the generation of the birth-pangs of *Mashiah*, in which outwardness holds sway, this way is still open to us. We can put intensive effort into Torah study in all its profundity, and through this, with God's help, we can arrive at inner enlightenment. We have one advantage: one who has been "outside" appreciates all the more the honor and glory of "inwardness." The same source, *Pirkey Heychalot*, remarks that "although the Divine Presence did not rest upon the Second Temple, Torah learning in all its splendor and glory flourished only in the time of the Second Temple." ☐

notes

1 See p. 176.
2 *Bamidbar Rabba Ḥukkat*, 19:3.

3 *Shemot Rabba* 52:2.

4 *Ḥagiga* 4a.

5 R. Mosheh ibn Ezra, *Shirat Yisrael*, p. 154, based on *Berachot* 6b.

6 Sec.2, para. 26.

7 For further discussion of this point, see pp. 187-188. For a recommended method of achieving it, see pp. 208-209.

8 *Shabbat* 133b.

9 *Yoma* 75a.

10 *Menaḥot* 29b.

11 *Pesaḥim* 50a.

12 *Bereshit Rabba* 61:1.

13 *Michtav Me-Eliyahu*, Volume II, pp. 27, 39.

14 *Tikkun* 40.

15 *Nedarim* 38a.

16 *Menaḥot* 29b.

□□□□□□□□□□□□□□□□□□□□□□□□□□□□□□□□□□□□□□

This was sent from England to the Ponevezh Yeshiva early in 1948.

Mitzvot as "life" and mitzvot as "apparel"

□□

We find that mitzvot are sometimes called "life," as we say in our prayers "for they [the words of the Torah] are our life." In other sources, however, we find that mitzvot are called *levushim* (apparel). What is meant by these terms, and do they not involve some contradiction?

The truth is that there are two ways of performing mitzvot.

(1) One can perform a mitzva with inwardness of heart, with feeling, with struggle against the *yetzer ha-ra'* and with self-sacrifice. This is what is called "life," since it adds to the personality a point of holiness which was not there before. "Living" means supplying a need which the ego feels and struggles to fulfill[1] — and this is what has been done in this case.

(2) Another way of doing mitzvot is as a result of one's upbringing, as "human commands learned by rote."[2] This is the type of mitzva performance called "apparel." Even if it is lacking in inwardness it has considerable educational value, and can prevent a person from falling still lower. One who is surrounded by mitzvot possesses a certain shield against the *yetzer*

ha-ra', even if they are done only outwardly and super-
ficially. This is why they are called "apparel"; clothing
is a safeguard against the environment. This is the
holiness that resides in the mere performance of mitzvot, even for extraneous motives.

TRUE MOTIVATION

But it seems difficult on the face of it: how can an act be
considered as the service of Hashem without proper
motivation? And can there be holiness without true
service? The answer is, as we have stated above, that the
act itself has its effect on us by way of safeguard — and
this, too, is the will of Hashem. But this cannot be
called "life." A person can be said to live spiritually
only when there is renewal and growth in his inner
essence. (We find that Yehoshua' the High Priest, in
the early days of the Second Temple, was punished for
not doing enough to prevent his sons from marrying
unsuitable wives. In the vision of Zechariah, he
appeared before the angel dressed in filthy garments.[3]
The "garments" symbolized the outward mitzvot he
had done, which were affected adversely by the *hillul
Hashem* in which he — however indirectly — had been
involved. Being a cause of desecration of the Divine
Name has an adverse effect on the personality. This
works in the opposite direction in relation to the holiness usually produced by such mitzvot. Later, when his
sons repented and separated from their wives, the angel
was told to "remove the filthy garments from upon
him."[4]

"God made man in His image."[5] Just as God renews
creation every day, so should man renew his inner

being, his feelings and alertness, which constitute his inner life. We must look at this in its deeper psychological aspect. Sometimes one resolves to strengthen oneself in Torah and mitzvot, but after a short while one's resolve fails and one finds oneself in the same state of slackness as before. "Who can ascend the mountain of God?"[6] — this is hard enough in all conscience; but "who can *stand* in His holy place?" — to remain there after one has reached it is the hardest task of all. The *yetzer* will come up with plots and intrigues of all kinds to throw the person down from his high position, some of them demonstrating intimate knowledge of psychological factors.

Let us consider a few of them.

WILES OF THE YETZER

If we try to push a nail into a wall, we shall not succeed. Neither will one hammer blow achieve it. But successive blows with a hammer will get it in. The *yetzer* adopts similar tactics. It attacks and withdraws again and again. We see this in the case of the man who has resolved to give up smoking because he suffered severe chest pains during the night. The next morning, when the first craving for a cigarette arises, he says to himself, "No, I am definitely not going to smoke. I had chest pains, didn't I? And I made up my mind not to smoke." The craving will leave him for a short time. But it will soon return with renewed vigor. He may reject it a second time. But it will keep on coming back, stronger each time, until he gives in. The reason, says Rabbi Simḥa Zissel, is that when the craving was rejected, the desire was not eliminated, but only suppressed. The second prompting was reinforced by the memory of the first. This is why the attacks become progressively stronger. Similarly, when the person "took himself in hand" and resolved to exert himself to the full in Torah and mitzvot from now on, the *yetzer* was only suppressed and it continues to remind the person of the pleasures of laziness. The memories of all previous attacks reinforce each new one, until they are strong enough to overthrow his resolve completely.

Another tactic is to mislead the person into thinking that when he has defeated the *yetzer* on one occasion, he has nothing to worry about. The *yetzer* will then attack him and defeat him when he is off his guard. The joy of victory becomes the weapon of the *yetzer*.

Sometimes a person may ascend the mountain and even remain standing in the holy place. He has resolved to undertake high quality observance of some part of Torah and mitzvot and he perseveres in his resolve. He imagines he has made a breakthrough. He has defeated the *yetzer* and his victory is complete. But the *yetzer* is cunning and snatches victory from the jaws of defeat. The very fact that the person can now keep Torah and mitzvot without hindrance means that he has lost the essence of what he is striving for. The "living" quality of Torah and mitzvot depends on constant struggle. Without this, they are but "apparel." To be "alive," one must be always alert, always ready to fight his *yetzer* and to stand the tests of life. Then his Torah and mitzvot may be called "true life."

If the *yetzer* cannot prevent you from doing mitzvot, it can prevent them from being "live" mitzvot by letting you do them without effort and without difficulty. A person easily follows this path, and is so happy with all the good deeds he is doing without having to fight his *yetzer*. He thinks they are earning him eternal life, and it never occurs to him to wonder: Why is everything so easy for me? Why have I no tests? Where is my *yetzer ha-ra*'? He may then make the further mistake of thinking that he is a *tsaddik* and *hassid* since he does so many good deeds. And then he is in real trouble, since arrogance is like idolatry.[7]

The Rabbis say, "Better once with effort than a hundred times without."[8] The reason may be that "without effort" means "without overcoming a test," in which case the mitzvot are without life. It may be appropriate here to mention what we have cited in another article[9] about the report of Rabbi Yose that in his time there were bandits in the mountains who spared Jewish wayfarers. Rabbi Yose says that in this merit they are "*'Olam ha-ba* people." From this we see that anyone who overcomes *his particular temptation* and conquers his *yetzer* on *his own behira-level* has arrived at a point of spiritual life.

TWO PATHS

There is another saying of our Rabbis: "Sabbath and circumcision were arguing...Sabbath said, 'I am greater'...circumcision said, 'I am greater'...When we see that circumcision has the power to set aside the Sabbath, we see that circumcision is greater."[10] We know that the principle of Sabbath, based on the seven days of Creation, is the principle of introducing the spiritual into the material, while that of circumcision is superseding the material altogether. It is clear that both these paths are essential for spiritual progress. The question is: Which has precedence? The answer given is that the latter has precedence. This leads to some surprising conclusions.

There are a number of cases in the Torah where the mitzva comes to sanctify the things of this world. A blessing permits the subsequent enjoyment, separation of *teruma* and *ma'aser* permits consumption of the rest of the crop, the giving of charity justifies the possession of wealth,[11] and so on. The principle behind these mitzvot is that a person's main striving should be for the mitzva; the enjoyment should be a mere accessory of the mitzva (and also a means to help one do many more mitzvot). This means that a person should try to reach the *madrega* where his main striving is to bless his Creator; he accepts the pleasures of this world *only* so that he can feel deep gratitude in the blessing that he makes. Similarly with other mitzvot of this kind, such as *'oneg Shabbat*, whose main purpose is to make *the Sabbath* pleasurable; that is, the good food and fine clothes should impress his mind with the sublime glory of the spiritual ideal of *Shabbat*. But the *yetzer ha-ra'* can misuse these mitzvot by making the physical pleasure our only goal, thus using the mitzva to "cover up" the evil. Thus it succeeds in turning holiness into defilement; the defilement exists because of the mitzva which condones it. Rabbi Yisrael Salanter said about this, "You can eat up the *Shabbat* in the *tsimmes*."[12]

How can one fight against this? Only by transcending physical strivings and "breaking" one's desires. Only if we are able to transcend the physical can we expect to succeed in penetrating the material with the spiritual. Otherwise, the whole enterprise is very dangerous. Defilement will rule our hearts, using the mitzvot to disguise itself. This is the meaning of the *Yalkut* we cited above which tells us that circumcision (transcendance) takes precedence over *Shabbat* (penetration). How many secrets of the human soul do *Hazal* reveal to us by this little parable!

And here, too, we can see the vast difference between mitzvot which are "life" and mitzvot which are "outward apparel." A living mitzva, which is part of a person's striving to make progress in holiness, is much less prone to be misused by the *yetzer* in the way we have described. If the mitzva is just "apparel" (an act devoid of spiritual content), it is much easier for the *yetzer* to steal the outward raiment and use it to cover up the defilement of *tum'ah*.

SAFEGUARDS FOR INWARDNESS

We have found a most remarkable statement in the Torah commentary of Rabbi M. Recanati.[13] He says that a judge who is lax in making safeguards will not merit *'Olam ha-ba*. Now it is clear that this does not refer only to a judge; everyone is a judge concerning his own life. The point is that anything that a person makes the object of his innermost longings is obviously a matter of great concern to him. He will naturally worry about it and arrange all kinds of safeguards to ensure that he retains it. If a person fails to do this, it can only mean that his mitzvot are "external" ("apparel" and not "life") and there is no *'Olam ha-ba* in them.

We have explained in "Being and Having"[14] that eternal life in the spiritual world is determined by the interplay between realization of one's own unworthiness and the immensity of Divine love. If one's acts are "external" — even if accompanied by a point of inwardness — this means that there is an admixture of *shelo lishmah* in his motivation. ("Externality" and *shelo lishmah* are identical; a person's acts are "external" only because they are guided by motives other than pure *lishmah*.) *Shelo lishmah* implies a degree of separation from Hashem; the person has interests other than fulfilling the will of Hashem. To the extent that he fails to subject himself entirely to Hashem, he will not be able to feel his own unworthiness, and the dynamics of a spiritual life in 'Olam ha-ba will not operate, as explained in the article referred to. If a person fails to make safeguards to protect his spiritual life in this world, he clearly has not subjected himself entirely to Hashem and he will lack the ability to experience the 'Olam ha-ba process. This is the deeper meaning of Rabbi Recanati's statement.

□□□□□□□

We live in difficult times[15] and our obligations are many. Those whose *beḥira*-level — for the time being — is confined solely to concern for their fellow Jews are doing *their* mitzva with exemplary self-sacrifice, single-hearted idealism and tremendous resolve.[16] Where do *we* stand? What is demanded of us on our own level is spiritual devotion to Torah and mitzvot with the utmost inwardness of heart. What are we actually doing? Are we ready to devote ourselves singlemindedly to Torah and prayer with real inwardness? Maybe it is just this that is needed to call forth the salvation from Hashem. Firm resolve, both individually and communally, a spirit of cooperation, self-sacrifice in Torah learning, the outpouring of the heart in prayer — these are the factors that weigh most heavily with God, and they will hasten His salvation. □

notes

1 See "Being and Having," pp. 184 et seq.
2 *Yesha'ya* 29:13.
3 *Zechariah* 3:3 and Rashi ibid. See *Sanhèdrin* 93a.
4 *Zechariah* 3:4.
5 *Bereshit* 1:27.
6 *Tehillim* 24:3.
7 *Sota* 4b.
8 *Avot de-Rabi Natan* 3:6.
9 See p. 197.
10 *Yalkut Shim'oni, Yirmiya* 33; no. 325.
11 *Shemot Rabba, Mishpatim* 31:3.
12 Also see the next article.
13 *Mishpatim*, beginning, quoting from *Zohar Ḥadash, Ruth*.
14 See pp. 191-192.
15 Note the date of this article.
16 This refers to the predominantly secular youth of Eretz Yisrael. *Their* mitzva, as they understood it, was to defend their fellow-Jews in Eretz Yisrael, and this they did with exceptional bravery and self-sacrifice. The words "for the time being" hint at Rabbi Dessler's confidence that they too would one day return to the full range of Torah observance. — *A.C.*

Sent from England to Ponevezh Yeshiva, 1948.

The secret of temple-building — the offering of the heart

THE RAISING OF "HOLY SPARKS"

□□□

"And as for me my prayer to You, O God, is a time of goodwill."[1] "Goodwill" is that which proceeds from the service of the heart, complete self-sacrifice, the offering of one's whole ego to Hashem. This is the meaning of sacrifice and prayer. And this is what is needed for building the Temple.

"Nullify your will before His will."[2] It does not say "Bend your will," but "nullify your will," that is, not to want anything that is not His will. When a person distances himself greatly from his desires, he will eventually not feel any more desire for them. As Rabbi Avraham ibn Ezra says, the tenth commandment "You shall not covet," means that the prohibition of taking someone else's property should become so crystal clear that the very idea becomes an impossibility. The desire then ceases, just as the rough villager has no desire to wed the king's daughter.[3] (This is also hinted at in the verse which says "You are not *able* to eat the tithe of your animals in your home town,"[4] which means, as Targum Onkelos says, "You are not *allowed* to....") This is what is meant by "a time of goodwill" in the verse quoted above — when one has no will but to do the will of Hashem.

TEMPLE IN THE HEART

Rabbi Ḥayyim of Volozhyn writes that the true Temple is in the heart of man (as it says, "I will dwell within *them*").[5] The Temple which was built in Jerusalem was only an instrument serving that inner Temple. "Therefore when they corrupted the inner Temple the outer Temple was no longer of any use and was destroyed."[6] It follows that the building of the outer Temple must depend on the building of the inner Temple, which is the sanctity of the heart. And what is this? None other than the "time of goodwill" of which we spoke above.

The Torah takes up a good deal of space in describing Israel's voluntary gifts for the building of the *Mishkan* in the desert.[7] It is certain that their giving was with complete goodwill and great enthusiasm. We can have no idea of the intensity with which each member of Israel wanted to contribute to the building of the *Mishkan*, nor of the enthusiasm, desire and sublime devotion that informed this giving. We cannot imagine the happiness in the heart of each individual when he knew that his money or property had reached the hands of the treasurer and it was now certain that his silver or gold would be built into the *Mishkan*, that he would actually have a share in the House of God and the Divine Presence would actually rest on his voluntary gift.

But in reality this was not how the *Mishkan* was built. How then? The Torah says in this connection, "Take from yourselves a gift for Hashem."[8] Ibn Ezra remarks that "take" is usually the opposite of "give," but "taking for someone else" is the equivalent of giving. *One can notice here the undercurrent of great things.* A person may give for the right motives, his giving may be completely unselfish, but it may not be *taking* — he may not be *taking from himself*; he is not overcoming resistance in order to give. The problem is that when a person reaches the level of *lishmah*, of unselfish giving, his actual *service* of Hashem decreases. He is doing what he likes, while *service* means bending one's will to do what Hashem likes. How is a person a servant of Hashem if he is no longer "serving" Him in this sense? (We know that "an act is measured by the trouble involved in doing it"[9] and "man is born for toil."[10]) Rabbi Yeruham taught us that the purpose of free will is to outgrow free will and feel "compelled" to do the right.[11]

Where is the aspect of *service* in these high levels?

· BODY-SHADOW

We have already explained at length (in the essay entitled "Body-Shadow")[12] that even the greatest *tsaddik*, since he is alive in this world, still has in him something of this world. This may be true only to a very small degree, even to the minimal extent which we have called "the shadow of the physical" but it inevitably exists.

It follows that even when giving with great emotion and enthusiasm, somewhere in the depths of the heart there still exists a very fine point of real resistance on the part of the *yetzer*. Even if it is only in the nature of a shadow, it still constitutes an opposition to the good that we are doing.

Now we can have the answer to our question. Those great *tsaddikim* who always acted out of love, in what lay their toil, their onerous service of the Almighty? The answer is: Their dealing with the immeasurably fine points of resistance hidden deep in their subconscious minds. These are extremely difficult to detect and all the greatness of these great men is needed to discover them, fight them and destroy them wherever they are.

This is why the Torah says, "Take from yourselves." The Torah is saying to the members of that great generation: Look well into your innermost heart and find the fine point of *yetzer ha-ra'* which actually opposes giving to the *Mishkan* — and there you are to "take from yourselves." This is the service involved in the building of the *Mishkan* — service in the depths of the heart. *This is how the Mishkan was built.*

And further, on the verse *"kol nediv libbo,"*[13] Ibn Ezra points out that literally this would mean "everyone who is generous with his heart," while clearly the meaning is "everyone whose heart is generous." But looking at the inwardness of the matter, maybe this is just what the Torah is teaching us. *The Temple is built by giving up one's very heart.*

THE HOLY SPARKS

If we delve more deeply, we can learn from here the meaning of the concept of "raising the holy sparks" and the dangers involved in this activity. We are familiar with the idea of "*shelo lishmah* bringing one to *lishmah.*"[14] But we are mistaken about its meaning. It is not the *shelo lishmah* which brings one to *lishmah.* It is the point of *lishmah* (which is always present) that softens up the *shelo lishmah* and enables one eventually to eradicate the *shelo lishmah* entirely.

There is a duty to eat and drink on *Shabbat* — the mitzva of *'oneg Shabbat*.[15] There is a well-known passage of rhyming prose in *Sefer Ha-maor Ha-katan* by Rabbi Zeraḥya Halevi[16] in which he states that those who are overscrupulous and fail to keep their food hot overnight so as to enjoy hot food on *Shabbat* morning give rise to the suspicion that they may be heretics. [The Karaites considered this an infringement of the Sabbath laws.] On the contrary, he says, "He who prepares his food before *Shabbat*, and keeps it warm in the prescribed manner, so as to make the *Shabbat* as pleasurable as possible — *he is the true believer, and he will inherit eternal life.*"

I have always found difficulty in reconciling this with the statement attributed to my revered great-grandfather Rabbi Yisrael Salanter to the effect that one can easily eat up one's whole *Shabbat* in the tasty *tsimmes*.[17] But the solution is this. It is true that one *can* lose the point of *lishmah* in the *shelo lishmah*, but the opposite is also possible: the *lishmah* may soften up the *shelo lishmah*.

This is the meaning of the mystical "raising of the holy sparks trapped in defilement." We have to elevate the inward motives which have fallen and become externalized — that is, we have to energize the *lishmah*-points which exist in the midst of the *shelo lishmah*. There is a danger, indeed, that they may be completely lost within the impurity. But if a person tackles the matter with honesty, he will succeed.

The mitzva of *'oneg Shabbat* is to bring the spirit of the holy *Shabbat* into all one's physical pleasures and so sanctify them — that is, soften their materialistic aspects. *Shabbat* can then cast its influence over the whole week, drive out physical desires and destroy them. This is indeed a wonderful prospect!

THE MIRRORS OF THE WOMEN

This idea is made even more explicit in the *parasha* of the *Mishkan*, where we are told that Betzalel "made the *kiyyor* (ceremonial washing basin) of copper...from the [burnished copper] mirrors of the women who thronged the entrance of the Tent of Meeting."[18] Rabbi A. Ibn Ezra comments on this:

> It is normal for women to beautify themselves and to look at their faces in the mirror every morning...to adjust the adornments on their heads...But there were in Israel women whose interest lay in the service of Hashem and who turned away from the desires of this world; and they donated their mirrors as a freewill offering, since they had no further need to beautify themselves. Instead, they came each day to the entrance of the Tent of Meeting to pray and to listen to the explanations of the mitzvot. This is why the verse says "the women who thronged...," for there were many of them.

This was a prime example of the way gifts were given to the *Mishkan*: a giving with all one's heart — *giving the heart itself with the gift*.

No dimensions or weight are given for the *kiyyor* and Ramban[19] explains that it was made from as many copper mirrors as were brought by "the women who thronged." Rambam also comments:[20]

> The throngs were extremely large and the women gathered at the entrance *to donate the mirrors in the*

generosity of their hearts. The finely burnished copper was exceptionally beautiful, and therefore it was decided to use it for this vessel. When the women noticed this, they all came in ever-increasing crowds to donate their mirrors.

Truly great were the women of that great generation. Even the least of them had the merit of seeing more than the prophets and hearing two commandments from the mouth of the Most High. Here the Torah reveals by what merit they succeeded in having this special portion in the *Mishkan*. [This was the only case in which an entire vessel was formed out of donations from just one section of the people.]

THE EXCEPTIONAL GIFT

Ramban adds in his comment on this verse:[20]

> In all the work of the *Mishkan* they accepted ornaments from the women, as it says,[21] "The men came together with the women and brought bracelets, earrings, signet rings and girdles," and the last-mentioned, according to the Midrash,[22] is even more questionable; but in that case all the gifts were mixed together. To make an entire vessel out of ornaments whose ultimate purpose is to satisfy the *yetzer ha-ra'* — this Mosheh did not want, until he was given specific instructions by the Almighty to accept them.

And a little earlier, [quoting Rashi], he says:

> Mosheh was going to reject them [the mirrors] because they were made for the *yetzer ha-ra'*, but God told him to accept them. "These are more beloved to Me than all the rest, because by means of them these women raised up throngs of children in Egypt."

"These are more beloved to Me than all the rest..."; "in that case all the gifts were mixed together..."; this is the way to the tremendous achievement of building a *Mishkan*. The holy is added to the profane so that the power of the profane (the *shelo lishmah*) is weakened, and it becomes easier to rise to the offering of the whole heart.

Ba'al Ha-turim[20] takes the matter still further:

> The word *b'mar'ot* [here in the sense of "with the mirrors"] occurs four times in Tanach; once here and three times in the sense of prophetic visions. These women had turned away from the desires of the world and had given their mirrors as an offering for the *Mishkan*, and therefore the spirit of God rested upon them.

This is how one builds up one's heart to become an inner sanctuary. In this way, one succeeds in building the vessels, the *Mishkan* and the Temple here below.

□□□□□□□

Someone drew my attention to a wonderful point. The Rabbis tell us[23] that Betzalel asked Mosheh Rabbenu: If the ark and the other items of furniture are to be made before the *Mishkan* itself, where are they to be put while the *Mishkan* is being constructed? And Mosheh agreed and said, "You must have been in the shadow of God." But the question still remains: Why in *Parashat Teruma* are the instructions for the ark given *before* the instructions for the *Mishkan* if, in fact, the latter is to precede the former? And anyway the ark is not subject to the limitations of space, as the Gemara says, "The ark did not occupy any space in the Holy of Holies."[24]

The answer is that, in practice, Betzalel was clearly right; one doesn't make the furniture before the house. But on the inner level, the ark must come first; the "point of inwardness" must precede its outward garments. The point of *lishmah* must be the factor which leads one to use the *shelo lishmah* and not vice versa. This is why the ark had to be mentioned first in the instructions. There is no need to elaborate. □

notes

1 *Tehillim* 69:14.
2 *Avot* 2:4.
3 Commentary on *Shemot* 20:14. See Volume II, p. 88.
4 *Devarim* 12:17.
5 *Shemot* 25:8.
6 *Nefesh Ha-ḥayyim* I, 4, gloss.
7 *Shemot* 35:30-36:7.
8 Ibid. 35:5.
9 *Avot de-Rabi Natan* 3:6.
10 *Iyov* 5:7.
11 See Volume II, pp. 62, 67.
12 Volume II, p. 208.
13 *Shemot* 35:5.
14 See Volume I, p. 96 et seq.
15 *Shabbat* 118a.
16 On the Rif, *Shabbat* chap.3.
17 Cf. above, p. 48.
18 *Shemot* 38:8.
19 Ibid. v. 21. Also Ibn Ezra, v. 8.
20 Ibid. v. 8.
21 Ibid. 35:2.
22 Ibid. See Rashi.
23 *Shemot* 38:22. See Rashi on *Shemot* 35:2.
24 *Yoma* 21a.

The Power of
the Yetzer

□□□□□□□□□□□□□□□□□□□□□□□□□□□□□□□□□□□□

These three talks were given at Ponevezh Yeshiva,
Ellul 5713 (1953), a few months before Rabbi
Dessler's *petira*.

Blockage of the heart

□□□

Every member of Klal Yisrael possesses a point of inwardness which can never be extinguished. This is the spiritual meaning behind the words, "I have never rejected them nor cast them out to utterly destroy them."[1] This derives from the promise given to Avraham Avinu in his covenant with God: ["I will establish My covenant with you and your children after you so that I shall be God to you and to your children after you forever."][2] This means that "the holy point" of attachment to Hashem will never cease to exist in the hearts of the people of Israel throughout all the exiles. God will never allow them to fall into spiritual annihilation and its consequence — physical annihilation, God forbid.

But we are told that "a little light can do away with a lot of darkness."[3] Why then does this point of light not drive away the darkness of our *yetzer ha-ra*? Why is the *yetzer* so successful with us?

The answer is *timtum ha-lev* (blockage of the heart). There is something that seals off our hearts and makes it impossible for the point of light to enter. We sense the presence of light, we know about it, but the entrance to the ego — the source of all actions — is blocked. The point of light has some effect, but this is not sufficient to influence our actions.

SPRINGS OF ACTION

Rabbi Yeruham Levovitz once said that hearing *mussar* may take the enjoyment out of physical pleasures without necessarily changing a person's deeds in practice. After accepting the Kingdom of Heaven in *Keriat Shema'*, we say the blessing which begins, "True, firm and enduring are these words to us." If one has already read the *Shema* with intent to accept the Kingdom of Heaven, why should one have to confirm it in this way? We must conclude that though reading *Keriat Shema'* with full intent is certainly an inner achievement, it is still possible for one to revert to one's original habits. The acceptance may not have penetrated far enough to affect the springs of action.

There are degrees of inwardness. One may be aware of the truth in one's heart without the awareness becoming "enduring." This is still an "outward" awareness. We can see this very clearly when observing people's characters. Anger is certainly something that is felt inwardly, especially if the anger is intense. But still there are degrees, as the Mishna says,[4] "Some are harder to conciliate, some easier." The more intense the experience is, the more inward it is.

"Sin blocks a person's heart."[5] In fact, the sin itself is the blockage. The will to sin will not *allow* the person to become interested in anything that might deflect his mind from the sin. Rabbi Hayyim of Volozhyn[6] sees this in the prophetic pronouncement:[7]

Fatten the heart of these people,
Deafen their ears,
Turn away their eyes!
Lest they see with their eyes,
Hear with their ears,
Understand with their hearts
And return, and be healed.

This gives prophetic expression to the fear of the sinner that he might inadvertently see something which would lead him to *teshuva*.

What can the would-be *ba'al teshuva* do if in his heart of hearts he does not *want* to think, in case he might have to change? This is the essence of "heart blockage" — the determined resolve not to think, or anyway, not to think in such a way as to penetrate the heart. [We are talking here primarily about the person who has always been "religious." The *teshuva* at stake is the change from *outward* to *inward* Judaism.]

THE HOLY SPARKS

It is said that "the wicked are full of regrets."[8] In that case, why do they stay wicked? Because the regrets are as if insulated in a capsule; they never penetrate into the inner parts of the *rasha'*. "Every day a heavenly voice proceeds from Mount Horeb and proclaims, "Woe to people for the insults heaped on the Torah!""[9] Who hears this voice? Everyone hears it subconsciously. The faint stirrings of conscience which everyone experiences from time to time are the effect of this voice, says the Ba'al Shem Tov; and this is also the source of those "regrets" with which the wicked are filled. But these promptings to repentance are not inwardly absorbed.

Even the momentary stirrings that they occasion are not "an arousal from below;" they do not amount to "an opening as the eye of a needle" to qualify for an influx of heavenly aid.[10] They are not the results of the person's own effort, and usually fade away and disappear very quickly.

Yitzḥak Avinu loved his son 'Esav *ki tsayid be-fiv*,[11] which may be translated as "because trapping was in his mouth." Rashi explains that he trapped his father with the words of his mouth, asking "religious" questions, such as "how does one give *ma'aser* from straw . . . from salt?"[12] But, says the great kabbalist, Rabbi Yitzḥak Luria,[13] this does not mean that 'Esav was a mere charlatan. It is not to be thought that Yitzḥak Avinu, who was a prophet of God, could be taken in by tricks of this sort. The word *tsayid* may be translated as "that which is trapped." It refers, says the Arizal, to the holy sparks trapped by 'Esav. If he had swallowed them he would have become a *tsaddik*. But he preferred to keep them in his mouth, and so remained a *rasha'*.

The holy sparks referred to here are the promptings to holiness which everyone experiences on occasion, and which 'Esav experienced with great force when he was in the presence of his father. At these times he was *sincerely* interested in how one gives *ma'aser* from straw, etc. He spoke about these matters with his father and with others, as one speaks about things in which one is outwardly interested. But his interest remained superficial; and in fact, the more he spoke about them the more superficial they became. (We have already referred to the fact that moral and spiritual insights are dimmed by communicating them to others; as the Talmud says, even a worry can be lessened by talking about it to others.[14] 'Esav's tragedy was that he refused to "swallow" the spiritual insights that were so close. He would only talk about them, and so they remained outside the "active ego."

□□□□□□□

It follows that those of us for whom *mussar* insights and promptings to repentance remain only in our mouths — subjects to talk about — are colleagues of 'Esav *ha-rasha*'. May Hashem save us from this fate and help us to break through the blockage of our heart. □

notes

1 *Vayikra* 26:44. See p. 21. Also see Volume I, p. 180 and Volume II, p. 132.
2 *Bereshit* 17:7.
3 R. Menaḥem b. Zeraḥ in *Tseda La-derech*, no. 12.
4 *Avot* 5:11.
5 *Yoma* 39a.
6 *Nefesh Ha-ḥayyim*.
7 *Yesha'ya* 6:10.
8 See *Nedarim* 9b.
9 *Avot* 6:2.
10 This concept is explained at length in Volume I, p. 103-4.
11 *Bereshit* 25:28.
12 Ibid., Rashi, verse 27.
13 Known as the Arizal (16th century).
14 See p. 36.

Obstinacy

□□

A person may reject the promptings of his *yetzer* without actually getting rid of it — without killing it. In this case, even if he succeeds in overcoming his *yetzer*, the effect will be like pressing down on a spring. The greater the pressure, the stronger will be the resistance. This may give us some insight into the principle "the greater the person, the greater is his *yetzer*."[1]

Pharaoh said, "God is just and I and my people are wicked,"[2] and no doubt he thought he was sincere about this. (We cannot believe he was merely trying to deceive; the Torah does not present lies as truth.) And yet soon after, "he hardened his heart,"[3] and eventually, as Rambam writes,[4] found the way to repentance completely blocked. The explanation is that since he did not get rid of his *yetzer* completely but merely suppressed it, his natural obstinacy asserted itself all the more and caused him to harden his heart. This is the spring effect we noted before.

REGENERATION OF EVIL

We found a most extraordinary statement in Rabbenu Bahya's commentary on the verse "they and all that was theirs went down alive into She'ol."[5] He writes:

> It says in *Tehillim*:[6] "The wicked shall *return* to She'ol."
> Why "return"? This hints at the idea that after being
> consumed by the fires of Gehinnom they are restored
> to their original state, so that they can again be con-
> sumed, and so on for generations.

This means that the spring effect applies not only in
this life but in Gehinnom, too. After the defilement
acquired in this world is burnt out by the fires of
Gehinnom,[7] what is left? The root of the defilement is
left, and that has the power to regenerate the evil. But
this applies only to that *rasha'* who in this world is
affected by the evil of obstinacy. All defilements are
burnt away in that world — except obstinacy. This
remains in spite of the burning. (One might say that
this is the counterpart in the sphere of *tum'ah* to the *luz*
bone in the sphere of *kedusha*, which can never be
destroyed and serves to regenerate the person at the
time of resurrection.)[8] Out of this root, the *tum'ah* is
regenerated in its original state and needs to be burnt
away all over again. And so on.

With the ideas discussed here we can arrive at a fresh
and wondrous insight. We shall develop this point by
point.

BEHAVIOR FOLLOWS HEAVENLY INPUT

(1) Hashem conducts the world with His attributes
of lovingkindness and strict justice. When strict justice
prevails, people become deprived and hungry, and
they, too, learn to act towards one another with harsh-
ness and anger. Theft, violence and murder increase;
refinement and courtesy disappear. People quarrel over

the slightest thing, nerves are on edge, there is no satisfaction. Everyone is strict with everyone else. On the other hand, when Hashem conducts the world with lovingkindness, plenty and affluence appear. People act with courtesy and refinement, honesty prevails, nerves are quiet; everyone is at ease with his neighbor. (It seems that here, too, we have an example of "man being created in God's image";[9] man's behavior reflects God's guidance of the world.)

(2) But when *ḥesed* prevails, there is a price to pay. Self-indulgence increases with affluence; people find it easier to gratify their desires. (Sexual permissiveness is defined in *kabbala* as distorted *ḥesed* of the sphere of *tum'ah*.)[10]

(3) The Talmud tells us that God is "angry" with the world for a brief time every day.[11] That is, each day the world needs a certain input of strictness and deprivation to preserve an equilibrium in human behavior. Bil'am's expertise lay in determining the precise moment of that "anger," which he could then exploit to curse Israel;[11] perhaps because at that moment he could develop maximum concentration on hatred and malediction. The Gemara continues:[11]

> The prophet [Micha] said to Israel, "My people, remember what counsel Balak…gave, and what Bil'am… replied in order to know the kindness of Hashem…"[12] God said to Israel: You should know what great kindness I did to you that I was not angry during those days when Bil'am was trying to curse you…as it says, "How can I bring anger when God was not angry?"[13]

But Bil'am was able to exploit this lack of anger, too. Since the anger of God was not felt during those days, it became easier to exploit the natural tendencies of desire. That is why he says, "And *now*...let me advise you";[14] now is the time to devise a plot to involve them with the daughters of Moab.

OBSTINACY AND IMPUDENCE

(4) Once the equilibrium had been disturbed by the absence of strictness and they had fallen into the trap so carefully laid for them by Bil'am, strictness was once again the order of the day and the plague struck.[15] In addition, they witnessed the energetic action of the courts hastily convened by Mosheh to execute those who had worshipped Pe'or.[16] The attribute of strict justice was operating — both from above and from below. And yet — in the midst of all this — Zimri flaunted his Midianite paramour "before the eyes of Mosheh and before the eyes of the congregation."[17] ("*He said, 'Mosheh, is this woman prohibited or permitted; and if prohibited, why did you marry a Midianite?'*")[18]

Zimri defied the plague and the punishment because obstinacy learns nothing from punishment. On the contrary, punishment only serves to reinforce it. The response of obstinacy is, "I will do it all the same, even if it costs my life."

(5) "They [Mosheh and the Sanhedrin] were weeping."[17] "The *halacha* had escaped them."[18] Zimri was not liable to the death penalty; he was not guilty of idolatry. It was also not appropriate to have him put to death by the emergency powers of the Sanhedrin.[19] In a situation where obstinacy rules, such action would only add fuel to the flames. (We must remember that

Zimri's act was itself the result of the rebellion of the tribe of Shim'on who looked upon him as their leader. "They said, 'We are being condemned to death and you sit idle...?'")[18]

(6) This also explains why Zimri was not struck down by God's justice and did not die in the plague. Even if they had seen this happen, they still would not have learned their lesson. Obstinacy is so terrible, the "spring" is so powerful, that this would have had the opposite effect. God considered it preferable, therefore, to leave Zimri unscathed rather than allow the "spring effect" of obstinacy to be revealed in all its starkness. [By leaving Zimri alive the way was left open for Pinḥas to solve the problem in his own way.]

(7) The only remaining alternative — the one in fact taken by Pinḥas — was to adopt the unusual course of "the zealous ones strike him down."[20] This is not a sentence of any court; it is not a deliberate judgment at all. It is an act of private zeal on the part of someone who cannot bear to see the Name of God profaned. God calls it "acting out the anger which I should have had Myself."[21] Since Israel saw it as an act of private passion and not a judgment from God, it did not initiate the "spring effect" and deflected their rebelliousness from the Almighty onto Pinḥas himself. This saved the situation. □

notes

1 *Sukkah* 52b. I.e., the greater the person, the more he suppresses his *yetzer ha-ra'*. As a result, the *yetzer* will return with redoubled force as soon as the "spring" is released.

2 *Shemot* 9:27.
3 Ibid. v. 34.
4 *Hilchot Teshuva* 6:3.
5 *Bamidbar* 16:33.
6 Ibid. 9:18.
7 The deeper meaning of this concept is discussed later in this volume. See pp. 206 et seq.
8 See *Vayikra Rabba* 18:1. For the meaning, see *Michtav Me-Eliyahu*, Volume IV, p. 155.
9 *Bereshit* 1:26.
10 See *Vayikra* 20:17.
11 *Berachot* 7a.
12 *Micha* 6:5.
13 *Bamidbar* 23:8.
14 Ibid. 24:14.
15 Ibid. 25:3.
16 Ibid. vv.4-5.
17 Ibid. v.6.
18 Rashi ad loc. from *Sanhedrin* 82.
19 See *Yevamot* 90b.
20 Rashi on *Bamidbar* 25:7.
21 Rashi on *Bamidbar* 25:11.

The power of evil

The *yetzer ha-ra'* is not a mere illusion. It is a created power: "He forms light and *creates darkness*."[1] "It is no ordinary creature"; the Rabbis call it an "angel,"[2] i.e., a messenger from God. But at the same time it is an object of idolatry — the "strange god stationed in the heart of man"[3] it is "situated at the entrance of the heart"[4] to prevent the entry of holiness. It is also called a "king" — it certainly dominates the world; "old" — experienced in cunning; "angelic" — superior to all worldly power.

Hester panim — the hiding of the Divine Presence — means that the conduct of the world is, apparently, surrendered by Heaven to the Other Side. Heaven conducts the world in accordance with the will of the Other Side — the power of evil. This causes desecration of the Divine Name. "You forget the Rock that gave you birth"[5] is interpreted by our Rabbis to mean that the power of Heaven is weakened here below.[6]

In this situation everything that one sees teaches him the opposite of the truth. Real power — apparently — is given to the Other Side. "God *made* one to correspond to the other"[7] — there is a world of evil corresponding to the world of good. ("Made," in Hebrew *'asa*, alludes to the world of *'asiya*, the lowest of all the worlds. Here, in a time of withdrawal of the Divine Presence, it really looks sometimes as if an alien power were in charge.)

Rabbi Yeruḥam Levovitz used to say that the false prophets mentioned in *Tanach* were not mere liars and cheats. They had a prophetic experience, but the prophecy was false, coming from the Other Side. There is a prophecy of defilement just as there is a prophecy of holiness: "God made one to correspond to the other." [It is for the person himself to distinguish between them by activating the perception of truth in his own heart. Here the false prophets failed.]

Had they been mere cheats, the Torah would not have called them prophets. The Torah itself says, "If there should arise among you a prophet...and he gives you a sign or a wonder, and the sign or wonder comes true...with the intent that you should go after other gods...you shall not listen to the words of that prophet...."[8] Though he is clearly a false prophet, the Torah does not hesitate to call him a prophet without further qualification.

At the sin of the Golden Calf, *Satan* succeeded in inflaming the Israelites' imagination until they saw a vision of Mosheh's bier being borne aloft by the angels.[9] Although false, this was a quasi-prophetic vision. Under the influence of the evil inclination they had all temporarily become false prophets.

Concerning the Golden Calf itself, Rashbam raises the question of how the Israelites could possibly have said, "These are your gods, O Israel, who brought you up from the land of Egypt."[10]

Were they idiots? Did they not know that this newly-made "calf" could not possibly have brought them out of Egypt? Of course all idolaters knew that our God in heaven created the world. However, it was a fact of experience that *terafim* and similar artifacts conveyed messages by means of the spirit of defilement, just as true prophets spoke by means of the holy spirit. The "calf," too, conveyed messages by unholy means. Their mistake consisted in thinking that it operated by means of the holy spirit from on high. This is the significance of their exclamation, "These are your gods, O Israel, which brought you up from Egypt," meaning "the powers manifested in the Exodus from Egypt are present in this object; the holy spirit is in it; it is as if the holy spirit goes before it." Similarly, Lavan said of his *terafim*, "Why did you steal my gods?"[11] [meaning objects in which Divine power is manifest]. This power was granted to the "calf" by God in order to test them.[12]

In the *Rosh Hashana* and *Yom Kippur* prayers we say, "Therefore please God, grant honor to your people, praise to your righteous ones (*but at présent the Other Side gives honor and glory to the opposite*)...joy to your land, gladness to your city... the righteous shall see it and rejoice..." (*When?*) "When you remove the domination of evil from the world."

But at present joy and gladness go to the powers of evil; shame and hurt to the *tsaddikim*. Why? Because we are in a time when the Divine presence is eclipsed; the Shechina is in exile. Now is the time when the powers of evil are in the ascendant. But a time will come when "You, God, alone will reign" — the time of the coming of the *Mashiaḥ*.

And we say every day in *'Alenu*, "Therefore, O God,

we hope…soon to see the splendor of Your glory; to banish idols from the earth; to put the world right by the kingdom of the Almighty." *L'takken*, "to put right," also means "to repair." The world needs to be recast in a new mold. Before this, it is as if the Divine kingdom were (God forbid) broken in pieces.

The prophet Zechariah says,[13] "On that day [the day *Mashiah* comes] Hashem will be one and His Name one," on which the Gemara asks,[14] "Is He not one today, too?" One answer is that nowadays His Name is not read as it is written, but *then* "He and His Name will be one." Another answer is that today the blessing we make over bad news is not the same as the one we make over good news; *then*, they will be one and the same. In our opinion these two answers are basically the same. Today, God's true name — His quality of lovingkindness — is eclipsed, and consequently we make the blessing "the true Judge" over bad news. In the future, when it will become clear that even the apparently evil is itself a manifestation of God's goodness and love, there will be only one blessing, "He who is good and does good." But up to that time, until God "slaughters" the evil in the world, it is not possible to see that everything is good. It looks as if evil is an independent power, existing outside the love of God.

In our generation, for our sins, the situation is much worse. We no longer feel there are two powers in the world. *We tend to see one power only — the [apparently] all-powerful Other Side.*

We could make excuses. We could say that our inability to see is not entirely our fault. Maybe we should have learned, but in fact we did not. Maybe we can say, "It shall be forgiven the whole congregation of the children of Israel...for all the people have sinned unintentionally."[15] But there is also an aspect of deliberate intent. There is a hint of rebelliousness too. "I do not want to." "I can't do it." "I know it's wrong, but I'll do it all the same." (This is the attitude of the criminal who says to the witnesses, "I don't care if I am put to death for this; I will still do it."[16])

Let us search our *Yom Kippur* thoughts. Do we really ask ourselves, "Am I sure that I shall not waste even a few minutes of Torah learning tomorrow? After all, I know that one who can learn and does not is said to despise the word of God,[17] and I know the punishment for that, but...." "Am I sure that tomorrow, if I happen to hear a little *lashon ha-ra'*, I won't listen to it, let alone join in?" "Am I sure that tomorrow, should the opportunity arise, I won't think at all of other people's shortcomings? After all, I know that one who glorifies himself by someone else's disgrace — even in thought — has no share in the World to Come, but..."[18]

What will be our answer? "I can't"? Then what use to us is *Yom Kippur*? We haven't repented at all! And more: If we have given the answer "I can't," meaning, "I don't want to," we have betrayed our attitude of rebellion and deliberate intent. □

notes

1 *Yesha'ya* 45:7.
2 *Bava Batra* 16b.
3 *Shabbat* 105b.
4 *Berachot* 61a.
5 *Devarim* 32:18.

6 Ibid. See Rashi.
7 *Kohelet* 7:14.
8 *Devarim* 13:2-4.
9 *Shabbat* 89a. See also Rashi on *Shemot* 32:1.
10 *Shemot* 32:4.
11 *Bereshit* 31:30.
12 *Rashbam* on *Shemot* 32:4.
13 *Zechariah* 14:19.
14 *Pesachim* 50a.
15 *Bamidbar* 15:26.
16 *Sanhedrin* 41a.
17 Ibid. 99a.
18 *Yerushalmi, Ḥagiga* 2:1.

Repentance

□□

This important series on repentance is taken from talks given at Ponevezh Yeshiva from Rosh Ḥodesh Ellul 5713 until after Yom Kippur 5714, in the last few months of Rabbi Dessler's life.

Essay on repentance

1

risking one's life for teshuva

A very interesting remark occurs in *Reshit Ḥochma*,[1] "One has to adopt an attitude of fear, which is repentance." And this applies at all levels, as the author continues: "This can be the lower fear (*fear of punishment*) which corresponds to the lower repentance, or higher fear (*awe before the exaltedness of Hashem*) which corresponds to the higher *teshuva*."

The author seems to equate fear of Hashem and repentance. But surely these are two different concepts?

The answer is that fear and repentance are indeed essentially identical. Only one act of *teshuva* is involved. Someone who is afraid of bombs falling during a battle runs away automatically. It is as simple as that. In practice, the fear is the cause of the repentance: "When he sinned he cast away his fear of Hashem, and he must therefore readopt the ways of fear in order to repent" — *Reshit Hochma*. But they cannot in any sense be considered two separate acts of *teshuva*.

One might object that fear of Hashem and repentance are counted as separate mitzvot. The answer is as stated by Radvaz:[2] "When does one transgress this commandment (to fear God)? When one does any sin...and fails to turn his mind to repentance...he has transgressed this mitzva....If he does repent, even from fear of punishment, he has fulfilled this mitzva (i.e., the mitzva of fearing God)."

On the mitzva of repentance Radvaz writes,[3] "The mitzva is to repent, as it says, 'They shall confess their sins [to God].'"[4] He apparently considers the mitzva of repentance not to exist independently, but to be included in the mitzva of confession. In this he follows Rambam, who writes at the beginning of *Hilchot Teshuva*,[5] "In the case of all the commandments of the Torah...when a person does *teshuva* and repents of his sin, he is obliged to confess...as it says, 'They shall confess [to God]...what they have done' — this refers to verbal confession, which is a positive command." He does not mention repentance as a separate commandment. In the introduction to *Hilchot Teshuva* he states, "These *halachot* comprise one positive command: that one should repent of his sin and confess." Here, too, it seems clear that the mitzva of repentance is included in the mitzva of confession.

In chapter 2 Rambam writes, "The Day of Atonement is a time for repentance...therefore all are obliged to repent and to confess." But no separate command to repent is implied.[6] Rabbenu Yonah in his *Gates of Repentance*[7] writes, "It is a positive command in the Torah that a person should rouse his spirit to return in repentance on the Day of Atonement, as it says, 'You shall be purified of all your sins before God.'"[8] The mitzva "to rouse one's spirit" is in essence the self-arousal which we call the fear of Hashem.

AWE IN THE PRESENCE

"The beginning of wisdom is the fear of Hashem."[9] "Wisdom" is what one sees in one's heart. The feeling of awe that comes over one when he realizes the presence of God is the beginning of wisdom. Seeing God in one's heart is to have the Divine Presence near him. When the Rabbis said, "The Holy One blessed be He is called the heart of Israel,"[10] they were, of course, not referring to God in His infinite essence, which is beyond all conception. They were referring to that small part of His ineffable glory which He deigns to reveal to us. That is what we call "Hashem," and *that* is revealed first and foremost in the heart of the *tsaddik*. The Shechina of God is said to "dwell among them in the midst of their defilements"[11] — that is, to dwell in their hearts.

Reshit Ḥochma continues:

> One who wishes to progress in holiness will adopt *fear, which is the Shechina* — the living presence of God ... In connection with *tsitsit* it says "so that you remember" ... and the Zohar explains that one must remember the "whip" and the harshness of strict justice;[12] and nevertheless it continues "so that you shall be holy to your God." We see that holiness follows from *fear*. And the word *Elokechem* is used, referring to the Shechina. (That is, the name *Elokim* is the one that is

revealed in the lower world in the midst of obscurity; and this is referred to as Shechina, "dwelling among them in the midst of their defilements," as we saw above.)

Radvaz, too, in the passage we quoted above,[3] goes on to say, "...For there is a higher *teshuva* and a lower *teshuva*, corresponding to the higher Shechina and lower Shechina."[13] In Ellul and the subsequent Days of Judgment, the need is for *teshuva*. This means we have to build in ourselves a fear which will *force* us to flee from sin. We have to build in ourselves nothing less than the Divine Presence. How awesome! And how difficult!

THE ULTIMATE SACRIFICE

We shall set down here some of the awesome words spoken by Rabbi Hayyim of Volozhyn in one of the discourses he delivered during the *Selihot* days of the year 1812:

> Unfortunately we have become members of a sect for whom evil has become an unimpeded path, God forbid. A sinner of this type is so habituated to sinning, so immersed in the mire of evil, that *if he were to do complete teshuva he would be in grave danger of losing his life, God forbid.* Our Rabbis say,[14] Anyone who is involved in heresy and abandons it, dies. The Gemara asks, What about Rabbi Elazar ben Durdaya, who was involved only in immorality, and died when he did *teshuva?* Answer: Since he was extremely attached to it, it was like heresy. It follows that a person *who sincerely wants to repent*, but has become so habituated to a number of sins that they seem permitted in his eyes, will find it *extremely difficult* to abandon them; repent-

ance may even cost him his life. Nevertheless he must
be prepared to give up his life to save himself from the
traps and snares of evil. The Torah says, "You shall
return to Hashem your God ... with all your heart and
all your soul;[15] *even if He takes your soul (i.e., your life)
from you as a result of the teshuva, you still have to
repent.*

Why is repentance in such circumstances likely to have
fatal consequences? Rashi explains:[14] "If they repent,
they are likely to die quite soon, as a result of the
distress due to the suppression of their *yetzer.*" Their
teshuva presents such enormous difficulties that their
constitution cannot stand it, and they die.

But why does Hashem, who is always ready to fortify
the weary and helpless,[16] not help them to overcome
their difficulties? To answer this question Rashi adds:
"There is a Royal Decree upon them that they must die."
In other words, we are not to raise queries about this.

On this Rabbi Ḥayyim, in the same discourse, has
something enlightening — and awesome — to say:

> Incessantly repeated sins can block off all access and
> cut the connection with the Almighty ... In such a case
> it may be necessary to accept death in order to escape
> from the toils of sin ...

If we look carefully at this we shall begin to see the
answer to our question. It is true that "if we make an
opening but the size of a needle's point" Hashem will
respond by sending a great influx of heavenly aid.[17] But
this occurs only when the turning to Hashem — the
"needle-opening" — is absolutely sincere and inward.
Only then will it re-establish the lost connection and
enable Hashem to turn to us as we turn to Him. As the

prophet says, "Return to Me and I will return to you, says your God."[18] But the deadening effect of accumulated sins may prevent one's *teshuva* from being sincere enough to arouse the appropriate response from on high — the "Divine Return." In such a case the only remedy may be death. It is known that at the moment of death one sees with greater clarity than at any other moment of one's life.[19] This is the moment when the light of *teshuva* may shine with its full intensity. For such a consummation, death may be worthwhile.

THROUGH THE COMMUNITY

The Gemara tells us that, in the case of an individual, a heavenly verdict once "sealed" cannot be revoked; while in the case of a community, it can be revoked through repentance.[20] What is behind the idea of "sealing" a verdict? The Gemara deduces it from the verse in Yirmiya[21] which compares the sin of Israel to an indelible stain on clothing (Hebrew: *nichtam*). This is similar to, though by no means identical with, the Hebrew for "sealed" (*nehtam*). The idea is clear, however. The verdict becomes irrevocable when the sin becomes like an indelible stain on the soul.

There is a way out, however. In the case of a community, repentance is *always* effective. The mercies they arouse are enormous and their merits are extremely strong.[22] However ingrained our sins are, there is still hope. Even if we have come, God forbid, to the state envisaged by Rabbi Ḥayyim, and our connection with Hashem is broken, we can still gain repentance by making ourselves part of a community. If we actively join a community which is singlemindedly pursuing the goal of repentance, we can radically change our prospects. We can even hope for true repentance and a year of life and peace.

2   □□□

extremism — good and bad

We learned above from the words of Rabbi Ḥayyim of Volozhyn that, when necessary, one does *teshuva* even if it involves the ultimate sacrifice. *Teshuva* is not set aside, like other mitzvot, because of danger to life. The reason why the Sabbath, for example, is set aside in such circumstances is because "One must desecrate one Sabbath to save this person so that he will be able to observe many Sabbaths in the future."[23] But this does not apply in the case of *teshuva*, because without *teshuva* the person will remain with his sins. What good is life to him then?

Rabbenu Yona makes an equally eloquent pronouncement:

> For what purpose is a person created? Only to occupy himself with Torah...And if he is going to involve himself with such things [which disturb his learning] what good is life to him? He might as well not be in the world; he is worthless and his days are worthless... Since he is no longer learning Torah, why should his life be continued?[24]

We learn from all this that for teshuva *we need extreme self-arousal.*

REINING ONESELF IN

On the other hand, when one makes resolutions in the course of one's repentance, one must take great care that these should not extend too far above what is practicable in his present spiritual condition. If a person tries to jump above his *madrega* he will surely fall and his whole repentance will end in abject failure. True, his arousal, his yearning for *teshuva* and his remorse for his sins must tend strongly toward the extreme, but afterwards, on the practical level, he must force himself not to take on too much at one time, so as not to threaten his new-found spiritual strength.

This is how we must feel: Aspire to the extreme, but rein in our aspirations.

All limitations that are placed on mitzvot — such as not to disburse more than one-fifth of one's property as charity; not to spend more than one-third of the value to beautify a mitzva; to give precedence to one's life over the life of one's neighbor — all these limitations should be felt as halachic restrictions imposed on the person against his will. Woe to the person who in such circumstances feels happy that he does not have to do more! We are reminded of the Gemara[25] which tells of the future occasion when the nations of the world will ask to be given the Torah so that they can gain entrance to 'Olam ha-ba. God gives them the mitzva of *sukka*, but when the sun's heat disturbs them, each of them "kicks over his *sukka* and leaves." Even though the *halacha* states that in such circumstances one is not obliged to stay in the *sukka*, that kick is sufficient to deny them entrance into 'Olam ha-ba. We see that the attitude to mitzvot is all-important.

On occasion the *halacha* adopts certain leniencies in the service of the synagogue because of "inconvenience to the public" (*tirḥa de-tsibbura*). This needs explanation. Surely each Jew should be prepared to accept some inconvenience for the beautification of a mitzva? The point is that each person must work on himself to purify his aspirations and welcome the opportunity to accept the "yoke" of a mitzva. But in a congregation there may be some who feel the burden is too great. Even if they were to comply, this would spoil the spiritual rapport of the congregation. In any event, one should love every detail of his service of Hashem, even those he finds most onerous. The rule is: Aspire to all possible heights.

A PENETRATING LOOK

Mosheh asked God to "show him His glory."[26] Did he not know that "no man can see Me and live"?[27] An answer is given by Radbaz:[28]

> In brief: Mosheh heard the Divine voice as conveyed to the Interpreter, who then explained to him the meaning of the words. His request was that he should no longer require an interpreter...something quite conceivable at his level. The answer came: You cannot see My Face etc., that is, no human being can attain this level and remain alive. As soon as he reached it, his soul would remain attached to that ineffable experience without being able to part — "a love as fierce as death"[29] — and Israel needed Mosheh.

It is evident from this amazing explanation that, were it not that he was still needed down here in this world, Mosheh would have been quite ready to give up his life in order to attain an added degree of attachment to Hashem.

The receiving of the Torah at Mt. Sinai also involved this extreme sacrifice. All Israel then entered into this form of supreme attachment which might be called "entry into the fiftieth gate of wisdom," with the result that their souls departed from their bodies with each succesive word of the Almighty, and only by the dew of resurrection were they revived.[30]

In Ellul we have to take a penetrating look at ourselves. We have to see clearly what life is, what sin means, what the Day of Judgment signifies, and what is meant by the habitual sin which (God forbid) breaks one's contact with Hashem, as discussed earlier in this article. If we want repentance, we must not shrink from taking an aggressive approach.

3

spiritual influence from above

In the first part of this essay we quoted R. Hayyim of Volozhyn as saying that our efforts at repentance here below call forth a response from above. This is the idea expressed by the verse "… and I will return to you, says God." The meaning is that Hashem makes the light of *teshuva* flow into the heart of the would-be penitent.

The difficulty here is how to reconcile this idea with the concept of free will. Surely "everything is in the hands of Heaven except the fear of Heaven"?[31] True, we find in our prayers phrases of this sort, such as, "Compel our *yetzer* to be subservient to you,"[32] and

"Unify our heart to love and fear your Name,"[33] etc.
But these phrases also need elucidation.

We usually understand the idea of "heavenly aid" in
the sense that Hashem provides us with the "means"
by which to serve Him, as Rambam explains the prom-
ises of material blessings in the Torah.[34] This may also
take the form of a good environment, a good teacher,
and so on; but there can be no "heavenly aid" for the
inward act of *behira* itself. The act of free will must be
the person's very own.

But heavenly aid can also come in another form.
"Open for me a hole the size of a needle and I will make
for you an opening like the gates of the Sanctuary,"[17]
says God. And just as the "needle-point" refers to an
inward, spiritual reality — the complete penetration of
the heart's obstruction, even if to a tiny extent — the
Divine response must be of the same nature, i.e., the
"opening like the gates of the Sanctuary" must also be
an inward reality in the heart. This is not a limitation of
behira, but a consequence of *behira*. This is how the
world is run. A person makes a choice and bores a "hole
the size of a needle-point" into the obstruction around
his heart (and this is the needle-prick of *yir'at shamayim* which is solely in man's hands[31]), and the "great
gate of the Sanctuary" develops from this. This is
God's response to our actions.

When a person cleanses his heart, prepares himself
and begs God to enable him "to understand...to
learn...to do and to perform,"[32] or he petitions God to
"unify his heart to love and fear Him"[33] — this prayer
is itself the "entrance the size of a needle-point" which
is in man's province to contribute. *This itself is his act of
behira.* (On reflection we can see that *behira* lies essen-

tially in what one aspires to. A person *chooses what he wants*, be it the truth which hurts now but brings happiness in the end, or the falsehood of momentary, transient pleasures. Wanting something very deeply leads one to petition the One who can fulfill his desire. Thus, prayer is the direct consequence of *beḥira*.)

This can be a source of great encouragement to us. There is absolutely no reason to despair. We need only *begin*, and Hashem will complete our task. This is always true, how much more in these "days of goodwill" when we are told: "Search out God when He is to be found."[35]

4   □□□

communal repentance

1. The virtue of communal repentance

When assessing the value of communal repentance, the Gemara states that a community attracts "greater mercy, compared to an individual, whose merits are not so strong."[36] It is clear that they attract greater mercy because their merits are greater, that is to say, their repentance is of a stronger quality.

In another context the Gemara points to an apparent contradiction between the verse that states that God is close to Israel "whenever we call on Him,"[37] and another verse which asks us to "search out God when He may be found,"[35] implying that there are times when He may be found and other times when He is not so accessible. The answer given is that the latter verse applies to an individual (i.e., during the ten days from *Rosh Hashana* to *Yom Kippur*), and the former verse to a community, whose closeness to God is not time-bound.

An early Kabbalist comments:

> We know of course that God is near to all those who call upon Him in truth;[38] since God is ever-present and all-knowing, "near" and "far" can have meaning only in relation to man himself and his actions; it is his actions that bring him near and his actions that distance him [from God].[39]

It follows that an individual, however much he desires it, can never arouse himself to *complete teshuva* except during the Ten Days of Penitence, aided by the dread of judgment. A community, on the other hand, can *always* reach complete repentance; "their merits are stronger," as we saw above. (Unfortunately, in our days the dread of judgment no longer arouses us. But what else can we do but try our best to rally our spiritual forces in a communal effort during these days of judgment?)

FROM FREEDOM TO COMPULSION

We have written elsewhere,[40] in the name of Rabbi Yeruham Levovitz, that progress in *behira* consists of converting what was previously "free choice" into "compulsion." When one rises in *madrega*, one sees that what previously seemed to be an equally balanced choice was really no choice at all, for one alternative was true and the other false. One is now "compelled" to follow the truth, and the illusion of freedom falls away. *Beḥira* will however reemerge at a higher level. We also cited the *Siddur Ha-Gra* in support of this idea.[40]

It follows that there are two levels of *teshuva*. (1) In the first, one succeeds in suppressing desire for sin, but the temptation remains. Even after repentance the sin is still within his "*beḥira*-level." (2) In the second, one is cleansed of the sin completely; temptation ceases. One is no longer conscious of having "free will" to do the sin. With this insight, perhaps one can explain the somewhat obscure passage in the Gemara:[41]

> Rabbi Levi said: Great is *teshuva* for it reaches up to the Heavenly Throne... "up to" but not "including" [the Throne]...But did not Rabbi Yoḥanan say: Great is *teshuva* for it sets aside a negative command of the Torah, as it says:[42] "If a man divorces his wife...and she marries another, can he go back to her?...But you have gone astray...yet return to Me, says God?"
> There is no contradiction; one is speaking of the individual, the other is speaking of the community.

What is the apparent contradiction between the words of Rabbi Levi and those of Rabbi Yoḥanan? It seems that the "marriage bond" referred to by the latter cannot be reconciled with "up to but not including" the Heavenly Throne, mentioned by Rabbi Levi. There is no closer union than the marriage bond.

THE HEAVENLY THRONE

We can now interpret the parable. "Up to but not including the Heavenly Throne" refers to the type of repentance in which the revelation of God's glory is incomplete. We can resist the temptation, but the fact that the temptation is still there dims the glory some-what. This applies to the individual. But the power of communal repentance is so great that it can succeed in uprooting the temptation completely. This is the level corresponding to God's call "return to Me," as in the loving attachment of the marriage bond.

In the first section of this discourse we mentioned that an individual may, in extreme cases, find that his connection with Hashem is broken, and may some-times only be restored at the cost of his life. In the case of a community, however, the connection can always be restored by repentance; as the Rabbis put it, "the verdict passed on a community, even if sealed, can still be revoked."[20] [This can be understood along the same lines as the preceding.]

COMMUNAL SHAME

In Gemara *Berachot* 12b, we are told that "if a person sins and is then ashamed of himself, all his sins are forgiven." The Gemara wishes to bring a proof for this from a text referring to the people of Israel as a whole, but the objection is raised: "Maybe a community is different," i.e., maybe communal shame is more potent. This idea is interesting. At first glance, we should have thought that in a communal environment shame would be easier to bear and would therefore be less effective. The truth is, however, that this only applies to shame before fellow human beings. In the case of shame before the Almighty, the feelings of shame from a number of individuals who perceive themselves as a community can combine and form a potent force with the power to rectify all faults.

COMMUNAL SUFFERING

We have found a most extraordinary idea in the Gemara (*'Avoda Zara* 4a). The Gemara suggests that there seems to be a contradiction between the verse "God is angry everyday"[43] and the verse "Who can stand before his anger?"[44] The answer given is, "One is speaking of an individual and the other of a community." We have here another surprising concept. It seems that there is a great difference between an individual and a community in their ability to withstand suffering. An individual is always prone to query Divine justice, while the members of a community can be relied upon to learn from their punishment, and there is hope that it will lead them towards repentance.

When a person sees his sufferings in the context of the sufferings of Klal Yisrael, they are easier to bear and he is more likely to learn from them and repent.

2. *Reasons for the virtues of communal repentance*

One of the main reasons for the spiritual power of a community is the advantage given by *organization.* Organization is effective in spiritual life just as it is in mundane affairs. When people are linked by communal ties, they can more easily maintain their spiritual level.

This is extremely relevant to the service of Hashem in our generation, in which real inwardness is sadly lacking. The Zohar tells us that the powers of evil take on a different guise for each person in accordance with his ways.[45] And just as the *yetzer ha-ra'* approaches each individual differently, so do its tactics differ in each generation. Different arguments and very different approaches are used, with the result that each generation must vary its modes of defense accordingly. The Ethiopians tried to fight Italian tanks and airplanes with bows and arrows. I am not sure that we are any better. We face a formidable foe equipped with the most up-to-date weapons, with which he has already succeeded in conquering our whole generation. And our weapons are no better than toys. Let us at least adopt one of his favorite weapons — and organize! A concerted effort by many like-thinking individuals will at least give us a chance of success, with the help of Hashem.

We have already discussed, in connection with the sin of Achan,[46] the powerful effect of public opinion on the attitudes and behavior of the individual.[47] If a whole community is determined to maintain a certain spiritual level, it will not be easy for any individual to deviate from this. This is why communal repentance is so potent.

THE TSADDIK OF THE GENERATION

There is a further point here. "God saw that the number of *tsaddikim* would be few; He therefore planted some of them in each generation."[48] It is clear that each generation needs a *tsaddik* to learn from. His sincerity and purity of heart will influence all those with whom he comes into contact. This is natural, since "what comes from the heart goes into the heart."[49] Similarly, Rabbi Yehuda Ha-Nasi tells us: "The reason I am ahead of my colleagues is because I once saw Rabbi Meir from the rear; and if I had once seen him from the front I would have been still further ahead."[50]

This is another reason for the preeminence of communal repentance. In a community there is always at least one who is more spiritual minded than the rest, and his influence can raise the repentance of all.

COMMUNAL PRAYER

This idea serves to explain another related passage in the Gemara:

> Rabbi Ami said: A person's prayer is not answered unless he takes his life in his hands [with the prayer]; (*i.e., unless he prays with the utmost, self-sacrificial sincerity*)...But did not Shemuel explain...that [even when Israel said "we shall hear and we shall do" at Mt. Sinai] they were "insincere with their lips and lied with their tongues," yet "He being merciful atones for their sin"[51] (*so it seems that complete sincerity is not a prerequisite*)? — There is no difficulty: the first case is speaking of an individual; the second of a community.[52]

Rashi explains that the prayer of a community is heard by Hashem "even if *not all of them* are sincere," this clearly implying that at least *some* of them are, and it is they who can raise the level of all.

A MORE PROFOUND VIEWPOINT

One can approach this whole matter from a more profound viewpoint. There are seven points to be noted here.

(1) Before Adam's sin, the whole goal of creation was concentrated in Adam and his helpmate. If they had withstood their test, the purpose of creation would have been realized. As a result of the sin, the realization of the purpose was spread out over time, the six thou-

sand years of human history, and extended over many millions of individuals and innumerable acts of *beḥira*.

(2) Spiritual matters are not subject to quantitative increase. This can apply only to material things, which are the instruments of the spiritual.

(3) The breakdown of the original single *beḥira* into the acts of innumerable individuals implies a lowering of the world's spiritual level. It corresponds to the mixture of good and evil introduced by Adam's sin.

(4) As we know, each person possesses a unique admixture of psychological and intellectual qualities which form the basis of his own particular, unique contribution to the sanctification of God's name.[53] The *kiddush Hashem* resulting from all the acts of *beḥira* of all the generations combines to form the great *kiddush Hashem* needed to complete the purpose of creation, which remains unaffected by the numerical increase in participants.

In this world the main burden of "revealing God's glory" (*gillui kevod Hashem*) falls upon a united Klal Yisrael. In the World to Come, the nations of the world will also be associated, in a subsidiary capacity, in this great work; as we say in the prayers of the *yamim ha-noraim*: "And so may Your fear fall upon all Your works..." Every gentile in the world is destined to take part in this ultimate consummation of creation's purpose.

(5) Even before this final unification, *any* combination of persons engaged in sanctifying God's name can achieve great things. Unified *kiddush Hashem* is of a different order of magnitude, with greatly enhanced quality. And this is the more profound aspect of the virtue of a community.

(6) We can now see a different way of understanding the effectiveness of communal *teshuva*. The tremendous power released by their combined *teshuvot* penetrates the heart of each individual, thus creating a great combined revelation of God's glory. The broken connection is thereby restored.

(7) The prayer we referred to above continues: "May they all be formed into one band to do Your will with a perfect heart." All mankind will be united in one great orchestra of *kiddush Hashem* in which all parts will function with the utmost precision and perfection.

3. Individual repentance that counts as communal

There are certain animals that can regenerate a severed limb. We are all familiar with the process of healing wounds and injuries in our own bodies. The pattern of the whole must be present in each cell of the body, and this enables regeneration to take place. In the spiritual life, too, part of the community is present in each individual member, and this makes spiritual regeneration possible. Let us elaborate a little on this point.

When a *tsaddik* reflects on the deeds of the wicked, he learns from them. At the very least he learns how things should *not* be done. He learns, too, the evil consequences of evil deeds. He thereby rectifies to some extent the *ḥillul Hashem* those deeds created. The *kiddush Hashem* that is revealed to him in his heart in a sense counterbalances the defilement caused by the *rasha'*. This is what is called in *Kabbala* "raising the sparks of holiness from their exile." The defilement is no longer complete since it is rectified by the opposite effect it produces in the mind of the *tsaddik*. The revulsion he experiences when he witnesses the evil to some extent redeems that evil. Knowing the evil of evil is equivalent to knowing the goodness of good. The *tsaddik* is shocked and hurt by the desecration the *resha'im* cause in place of the sanctification they *could* have caused had they fulfilled the part allocated to them in creation. He thereby reveals that precise aspect of holiness that the *resha'im* could have revealed, had they elected to do so.

If someone is truly hurt by seeing someone else willfully desecrate the Sabbath, then that very pain reveals something of the true sanctity of the Sabbath — the sanctity that *could* have been revealed by the other person had he elected to observe the Sabbath in the first place.

"There were ten generations from Noaḥ to Avraham and all consistently provoked God…until Avraham Avinu came and received the reward they all should have earned."[54] This means that our father Avraham himself revealed all the *kiddush Hashem* allocated to the whole world during ten generations. He supplied all that they had missed, and thus "gained the reward they should have earned" — the spiritual potential they had failed to realize. This was achieved by Avraham through his character of lovingkindess. He loved the whole world and thus was united with all.

TWO MODES OF REVELATION

We have learned that "every individual has a share in *Gan 'Eden* and a share in Gehinnom; if he is meritorious, he receives his portion and his neighbor's portion in *Gan 'Eden*"; the contrary is also true.[55] The two "portions" are modes of revealing God's glory; one directly, by consciously choosing good, and one indirectly, by suffering the consequences of one's bad *beḥira*. This, too, can be a revelation of God's glory, since it reveals the precision and utter fairness of God's justice.

The neighbor referred to is someone in similar circumstances and with similar opportunities to his own, who chose evil instead of good. If in spite of the evil example of his neighbor's bad choice, he still chose good, the extra effort thus required doubled his *kiddush Hashem*. In the figurative language of the Rabbis, he gets his own share in *Gan 'Eden* plus the share he [the neighbor] could have had but chose not to take up.[56]

This idea is similar to Avraham Avinu's "gaining the reward they all should have earned." The difference is that Avraham achieved his results by love. He loved his fellow human beings with such a great and self-denying love that he was able to redeem the generations of evil. The tremendous revelation of God's glory that he achieved through this love supplied all the *kiddush Hashem* that should have been revealed by all mankind.

In this way, the spiritual level attained by one individual may sometimes be equivalent to that attained by a whole community, provided he is united with them in the bonds of love.

IMPORTANCE OF LOVINGKINDNESS

This is why it is so important, when preparing for *Rosh Hashana*, to perform as many acts of lovingkindness as possible. Even more, one should subdue one's ego in all one's dealings with one's neighbor, as we say in our prayers, "May my soul be as dust to all." My neighbor should be to me like a king, whose bidding I do gladly, "with mildness of spirit," without the slightest possibility of grievance or estrangement. Then my repentance will be a "communal" repentance. Even if one has become mired and enmeshed in sin, he will be able to find a way out — even in the midst of his life.

In the article "Day of Atonement,"[57] we quoted Rabbi M. Recanati as saying that the reason the atonement of the day depends on appeasing one's neighbor is because otherwise there would be estrangement between Jew and Jew. This would be at variance with the whole spirit of *Yom Kippur*. (The whole passage should be carefully studied.) But if so, it seems difficult to understand the *halacha* that a thrice-repeated attempt to appease the injured party is sufficient.[58] Surely if the person has not been appeased in fact, estrangement still exists?

This difficulty can be resolved by the idea presented above. Unity can be achieved by one side alone, even if the other side remains alienated, by the very fact that one has subdued one's ego in deference to the other and begged his forgiveness. The threefold repetition serves to fix this in one's mind, and the unity — on his side — is then complete.

ONE MAN'S TESHUVA

There is another aspect of this idea: that individual *teshuva* can count as the *teshuva* of a whole community.

The Gemara says: "Great is *teshuva*; even if one individual does *teshuva*, forgiveness is granted to him and to the whole world..."[59] This seems very surprising. How can the whole world be put right by the *teshuva* of one man? Maharal explains it thus:

> Since *teshuva* is above the world...[since] it was created before the world...[therefore] through *teshuva* the world reaches that level at which general forgiveness exists.... The individual who does *teshuva* opens a sublime gate, the gate of repentance, where general forgiveness is found.[60]

The meaning would seem to be that *teshuva* implies entry into a state where all is rectified. We have learned that repentance arising from love of God converts deliberate sins into meritorious deeds.[61] This occurs because the sin becomes a vehicle for the *teshuva* and is thereby redeemed and rectified. [Since the sin, ever present in the memory of the penitent, continually prompts him to deepen his *teshuva*, it has in fact been converted into a force for good.] *Teshuva* is "above the world" in the sense that it is above time. In a time sequence, the sin and the repentance are two separate events; how can one cancel out the other? But "above time," where past and present are one, the sin and the *teshuva* are considered together.

Now, since the generation and the environment in which one finds oneself certainly have their effect on a person, the more evil there is in that environment, the greater the value of his *teshuva*. It follows that the sins of the community are the vehicle for deepening his *teshuva*, and through this the sins are redeemed.

This may be one of the reasons we find the good so

often suffering along with the bad. Maybe it was in their power to redeem the wicked of their generation in the way we have suggested, and they failed to do so. The evil all around could have prodded them to deepen their *teshuva* and increase their merits to such an extent as to make all the wickedness around them a vehicle for their service, and so all would have been redeemed! What a responsibility!

5 □□

repentance through shame

Near the beginning of the *Seliḥot* service we read:

> Banished and gone are God's anointed priests
> Who know the worth of offerings and feasts.

The greatness of the *kohanim* lies in their knowledge of the *value* of the offerings. The highest spiritual level always depends on knowing the true value of things — both good and its opposite.

The *yetzer ha-ra'* adopts two different approaches: the open and the disguised. Sometimes it may arouse a very strong desire in a person, and tempt him to sin deliberately. And sometimes it may adopt a cunning approach, confusing the issue and playing down the gravity of the sin. It may suggest to someone who is devoting himself completely to Torah learning that it would not matter all that much if he were to take a short break — hiding from him the gravity of *bittul Torah* — wasting time that should be devoted to Torah.

BEING ASHAMED

We all know that we shall ultimately have to give an account of our sins, so why are we not ashamed of them? One reason is that we prefer not to think about them. Another is that the *yetzer* succeeds in hiding from us the true gravity of our sins. Learning *mussar* corrects both these faults and so enables us to feel shame for our sins.

"Whoever commits a sin and is ashamed of it has all his sins forgiven."[62] Not just *that* sin, but *all his sins*. If a sin is forgiven, this means that the impurity of the sin is removed. Thus "all his sins are forgiven" must mean that the whole person is inwardly purified; all the defilement caused by his sins disappears. Can this occur just because he is ashamed of one sin? Yes, it can. We are talking about a person who is deeply and inwardly ashamed before God for the sin he committed; it hurts him that he dared to transgress the will of his Creator. It follows that he has some conception of what it means to defy God, and how low a person can sink. If he truly feels this, he is already a changed person.

This is the meaning of the Maharal's comment:

> When a person is ashamed of a sin this means that he consciously rejects the sin...To feel ashamed of something is to distance oneself from it. This is in direct contrast to the insolent person who identifies with his sin, in which case the sin can never be dislodged...[63]

There is a remarkable point here. The Gemara we cited above[59] proceeds to derive the statement from the conversation between the spirit of the prophet Shemuel (who has been raised from the dead) and King

Shaul.[64] To Shemuel's question, "Why have you disturbed me...?", Shaul replies, "I am in great trouble...God answers me no more, neither by means of
prophets nor by dreams..." He deliberately omits to
mention the *urim* and *tummim*; he is ashamed to do so
because they need a *kohen* to convey their message and
he was responsible for the massacre of the *kohanim* in
the priestly city of Nov.[65] As a result of this reticence,
Shemuel informs him that "tomorrow you and your
sons will be with me"; true, they will die in the battle,
but in the future life they will be "with Shemuel," i.e.,
among the *tsaddikim*.

REJOICING IN JUSTICE

But according to another source,[66] Shemuel replies, "If
you flee you will escape, but if you accept God's justice,
tomorrow you and your sons will be with me... among
the *tsaddikim*." Avner and Amasa ask him, "What did
Shemuel say to you?" Shaul replies: "He said that
tomorrow we shall go to battle and be victorious and
that my sons will obtain great honors." Whereupon he
took his three sons with him and went out to the battle.
God called the ministering angels and said to them,
"Come and see what kind of creature I have in My
world! Usually, if a person goes to a banquet he does
not take his sons with him...but this man goes out to
war in the full knowledge that he will be killed and
takes his sons with him, rejoicing in the justice which
strikes him down."

It seems from here that his sins were atoned by
rejoicing in God's justice rather than by the sense of
shame. But the difficulty is only apparent. We can learn

from this the full significance of that shame that effects forgiveness for all one's sins. When a person is ashamed of his sins and filled with remorse, he is eager for a remedy and rejoices when he finds one, even if the remedy may involve his own death. Death means nothing to him compared to the remedy which enables him to partake of eternal life. He resembles a patient who is glad he has a competent surgeon who will carry out the dangerous operation which may save his life.

Every one of us has certain sins of which he is, at least, a little ashamed. Herein lies our greatest opportunity. Let us not brush them aside, but bring them to the forefront of our minds. If we reflect on them we may merit at last the beginnings of *teshuva*.

6 □□

confessing the truth to oneself

Confession means to confess one's sin *to oneself*; this is one of the most essential facets of *teshuva*. Maharal explains:

> To acknowledge one's sins is to completely slaughter the *yetzer ha-ra'*. By acknowledging one's sins, one gives oneself up to Hashem.... This leads to the complete removal of the *yetzer ha-ra'*, for where one is joined to Hashem there can be no sin.... Failing this, one might well return to the sin; this is how human beings act: they are inconsistent.... But when one confesses, "I have sinned to Hashem," one gives oneself completely to Hashem, and thereby completely removes the *yetzer ha-ra'* and attaches oneself to Him, Blessed be He.[63]

At the time of the Holy Temple, the *kohen gadol* used to make a confession on behalf of all Israel.[67] This seems extraordinary; how does Maharal's reasoning apply when someone else is confessing for me? We can learn from this that when a *tsaddik* achieves an elevation in level, he raises everyone else with him. When the *kohen gadol* experiences his unworthiness before God, each member of Klal Yisrael finds it easier to attain the same experience, and the individual *teshuva* of each finds acceptance. We have discussed this subject above, in section 4,2. This throws light on the function of the *sheliah-tsibbur*, who leads the prayers in the synagogue. It may also illuminate one facet of the meaning of priesthood. □

notes

1 By Rabbi Eliyahu de Vidas, one of the disciples of R. Mosheh Cordovero. Beginning of *Sha'ar Ha-kedusha*.
2 *Metzudat David* (*Reasons for the Mitzvot*), mitzva no.5 (Fear of God).
3 Ibid. no. 75.
4 *Bamidbar* 5:7.
5 *Mishneh Torah*, "Laws of Repentance" 1:1.
6 Many attempts have been made to explain why Rambam does not count repentance as a separate commandment. The most likely explanation is that Rambam considers it as an exhortation to return to the observance of the Torah if one has deviated from it in any respect. In that case, it is a mere reiteration in general terms of the requirement to observe all the mitzvot, and in *Sefer Ha-mitzvot*, rule 4, Rambam establishes that exhortations to observe all the mitzvot are not to be counted as separate mitzvot. Confession, however, is an aspect of repentance which could not have been deduced from the general exhortation, and therefore warrants separate listing. — *A.C.*

7 Rabbenu Yona, *Gates of Repentance*, Gate 2, § 14.
8 *Vayikra* 16:30.
9 *Tehillim* 111:10.
10 *Shir Ha-shirim Rabba* on 5:2.
11 *Vayikra* 16:16.
12 Zohar III, 145a.
13 The "higher *teshuva*" and "lower *teshuva*" presumably correspond to "*teshuva* out of love" and "*teshuva* out of fear" (see *Yoma* 86b). "Higher Shechina" would therefore mean "awareness of the Divine Presence awakening feelings of love" and "lower Shechina" — "awareness of the Divine Presence awakening feelings of fear." — A.C.
14 *'Avoda Zara* 17a. The story of Rabbi Elazar ben Durdaya is given in full in Volume I, p. 94.
15 *Devarim* 30:2.
16 *Yesha'ya* 40:29.
17 See Volume I, p. 103.
18 *Malachi* 3:7.
19 Zohar I, 218b.
20 *Rosh Hashana* 17b, 18a.
21 *Yirmiya* 2:22.
22 See below, part 4 of this section.
23 *Shabbat* 151b.
24 Commentary on *Avot* 3:10.
25 *'Avoda Zara* 2b.
26 *Shemot* 33:18.
27 Ibid. v. 20.
28 Radbaz, Responsa V, 319.
29 *Shir Ha-shirim* 8:6.
30 *Shabbat* 88a.
31 *Berachot* 33:6.
32 Morning blessings.
33 Blessing before the morning *Shema'*.
34 See Volume 1, p. 38.
35 *Yesha'ya* 55:6.
36 *'Avoda Zara* 5a.
37 *Devarim* 4:7.
38 *Tehillim* 145:18.
39 R. Menaḥem b. Zeraḥ in *Tseda La-derech, Hilchot Rosh Hashana* 1.
40 See Volume II, p. 67.

41 *Yoma* 86a, according to the reading in *Ein Ya'akov* and *Yalkut*.
42 *Yirmiya* 3:1.
43 *Tehillim* 7:12.
44 *Nahum* 1:6.
45 *Parashat Beshallah*; see *Yalkut Reuveni, Parashat Tetze*, end.
46 *Yehoshua'*, chap. 7.
47 Volume II, p. 194.
48 *Yoma* 38b.
49 See *Berachot* 6b.
50 *'Eruvin* 13b.
51 *Tehillim* 78:36-37.
52 *Ta'anit* 8a.
53 See Volume I, pp. 87-88.
54 *Avot* 5:3.
55 *Hagiga* 15a.
56 This idea is explained at length in *Michtav Me-Eliyahu*, Volume IV, p. 118.
57 See p. 125.
58 *Shulhan Aruch, Orah Hayyim* 606:1.
59 *Yoma* 86a.
60 *Netivot 'Olam, Netiv Ha-teshuva*, ch. 3.
61 *Yoma*, ibid.
62 *Berachot* 12a.
63 *Netivot 'Olam, Netiv Ha-teshuva*, ch. 5.
64 *I Shemuel* 28:15-25.
65 Ibid. 22:6-19.
66 *Vayikra Rabba* 26:7.
67 *Vayikra* 16:21.

We are far away — but do not despair

□□□

We are indeed far away from Hashem. We are weighed down, too, by our past; our good resolutions have never lasted long. Is there any point in hoping? "Sin deadens a person's heart," say Hazal.[1] And what of many sins, repeated year after year? We have never done *teshuva* yet. What is really the point of hoping?

The *yetzer* persuades us into thinking that what *he* wants is what *we* want. He infiltrates our very essence. We never hear him say, "*You* need to do such and such a thing"; it is always "*I* need...." On the other hand, we hear the voice of the real "I" — the spiritual "I" — always speaking in the second person: "Wake up, why are *you* sleeping...?" The *yetzer* has stolen our very ego. He has implanted in us a veritable *hatred* of our true selves and has induced us to love *him* — our mortal enemy. (See what Rabbenu Yona writes about this in *Sha'arei Kedusha, sha'ar* 1.) If we love *him* and hate ourselves, what possible affinity can we have with loving God?

Sometimes, in moments of spiritual effort or in prayer, we feel as if we need to envisage God in physical shape and form. This is because we see reality only in physical terms; we fail to appreciate the *spiritual* reality of other people or even of ourselves, how much less that of the Eternal Being! This thought, however, borders on idolatry. "You saw no image...."[2] But why don't we have this urge more often? Why doesn't the *yetzer* pursue us with this thought? Obviously because we are so far removed from any desire to get close to Hashem that the whole idea does not interest us.

But there is no need to despair. On the contrary, the farther away we are, the more God's love for us is made manifest. God's *ḥesed* is revealed with greater intensity in His care for the far away than in His care for the near. *Ḥazal* say, "In the place where *ba'aley teshuva* stand, *tsaddikim gemurim* cannot stand."[3] We have explained elsewhere that this is because the *tsaddik* gets where he is by his own efforts, while the *ba'al teshuva* receives new powers from Hashem, and thus reveals His infinite mercies to an incomparably greater extent.[4]

HOPE FROM THE SIDDUR

A careful look at our prayer book can give us much consolation and hope, however far away we may be.

(1) We commence the *Shemoneh 'Esreh* by calling God "*our* God." He allows Himself to be identified as "our" God — in spite of all our weaknesses, even our rebellion. How can that be? It is because He values our thoughts of *teshuva*, our *mussar* learning, our endeavors to find some spiritual strength in our prayers.

(2) We continue, "...and God of our Fathers...of Avraham...of Yitzḥak...and Yaakov" — exactly the same phrase as we use about ourselves! This is some-

what daunting when we consider the enormous gulf that separates us from our *Avot*. We may perhaps take some consolation from the fact that the *Avot* were not always so close to Hashem. As the Zohar says, "From a distant place He brought them near to Him... Teraḥ the father of Avraham and Naḥor...served other gods... and He took pleasure in them and brought them to Him from afar."[5]

(3) "The great, mighty and awesome God." His greatness — that is, His lovingkindness — is expressed above all in His love for the lowly. His might — in suppressing His "anger" against His wayward creatures and showing mercy to those very far away indeed. (We can learn about His attributes only by reference to our own.) His awesomeness lies in the inexpressible love He shows to those lowly and despicable creatures — ourselves. (We may recall the *piyyut* for *Rosh Hashana* which depicts God as receiving adoration from the heavenly hosts above, but "desiring praise" from lowly mortals here below.)

(4) "Who owns all." All is His; His glory is revealed in *everything that is*, without exception. In the *haftara* for the second day of *Rosh Hashana* we read: "I heard Ephraim bemoaning himself..." — "*mitnoded*," a little movement in the heart, a little self-arousal, and God already responds: "Ephraim is a precious son to Me...My emotions are stirred for him; I shall show him mercy, says God."[6]

(5) "And who remembers the loving acts of the Fathers and brings a redeemer to their children's children for His name's sake (*i.e., to reveal His attributes*) in love (*i.e., to teach us His attribute of love*)." He redeems us, the distant ones, as if in payment for the merits of

the *Avot*; but nevertheless His attitude to us will not be as one who helps out of a sense of duty, but "in love" — as an expression of *His* infinite and boundless love.

(6) "Who supports the falling." "God supports all the falling";[7] even one who is already in the depths of defilement and still falling will find that God, in His mercy, will support him. If he has only one spark of a good thought, Hashem will heal him from his dire disease and loosen all the cords with which his *yetzer* has bound him, until he is able to stand on his own with hope for the future.

(7) "And keeps faith with those who sleep in the dust." Even if we think there is no hope, holiness has left us, spirituality is dead and gone — but it is not so! The soul never dies; this is only a kind of sleep. Our Creator has promised us to revive the dead. And if bodily life can be regenerated, how much more spiritual life! Repentance is always a valid option. "I will put a new spirit within you."[8] "He keeps his faith with those who are [spiritually] asleep," and we can rely on Him and declare: "You are indeed faithful to revive the dead." Therefore: no despair!

GOD'S HOLINESS

(8) We declare too: "You are holy." Just as Your essence is "holy," that is, known only to Yourself and absolutely inaccessible to us, so too "Your *name* is holy." God's "name" refers to His conduct of the world, the attributes by which He is revealed to us. These too are largely inaccessible to us since they are too great and wondrous for our puny understanding to grasp.

(9) On the *yamim ha-noraim* we insert here a most extraordinary prayer. Having declared God's transcendent holiness we go on to beseech Him — "therefore," for that very reason — to make the whole world aware of His awesome presence. "Therefore" — since Your providence and conduct of the world are so far beyond the range of our understanding — "*therefore*, may Your awe spread over all Your works...*therefore*, please give glory to Your people...*therefore*, may the righteous see and rejoice, etc." What is the connection? A wonderful insight awaits us here. The climax of the prayer reads: "You are holy and Your name is awesome...and the holy God is sanctified in charity."[9] God's holiness is manifested above all in His unbounded love for us, His creatures; a love which is far beyond anything we can possibly estimate or imagine. That awesome gulf that separates creature from Creator, that awareness of holiness and transcendence, is expanded immeasurably — holiness upon holiness, separateness upon separateness — when we become conscious of His overwhelming love for us. [And "*therefore*" — just because of this — we can hope and pray that this glorious revelation be extended to the most distant and forlorn of His creatures.]

□□□□□□□

To sum up: Do not worry, however far away you may be; arouse yourself, make a move, and Hashem will bring you near. His ways are holy, and if we cannot grasp them, we trust in Him; He is trustworthy "to revive the dead." □

notes

1 *Yoma* 39a.
2 *Devarim* 4:15.
3 *Berachot* 34b.
4 Volume I, p. 103.
5 Zohar III, 98a.
6 *Yirmiya* 31:17-19.
7 *Tehillim* 145:14.
8 *Yehezkel* 36:26.
9 *Yesha'ya* 5:16.

Beginning is easy — why don't you begin?

□□

The Rabbis invite us to ponder the ways of God. They say:[1]

> Come and see, God's ways are not like those of human beings. If a human being says something to offend his neighbor, he may or may not forgive him...but if a man sins against God in secret and offers words of appeasement, God forgives him...and more: He thanks him for it; ...and more: He considers it as if the man had offered a sacrifice of bullocks; and not as an obligatory offering, but as a voluntary one, as the verse states: I will heal their wrongdoing, I will love them in a voluntary way."[2]

Maharal explains this Gemara as follows:

> God is thankful to him [the person who repents] because He wants the world to exist...and therefore [repentance] counts as a good deed for which gratitude is due...It counts too as if he had offered all the offerings...since the penitent offers *himself* to God. It is also called a "voluntary" offering because the sinner [in his own estimation] has placed himself [so to speak] outside the jurisdiction of the Almighty...He therefore [subjectively] has no obligations and whatever he does resembles a voluntary act, and God treats it accordingly.[3]

This seems surprising since it implies that the sinner, though punished for his sin, is not punished for failing to do *teshuva*. On the other hand, Rabbenu Yona, at the commencement of his great work on repentance,[4] emphasizes the grave and cumulative responsibility of delaying repentance even by one day. He compares this to the prisoner who is shown an escape tunnel and fails to take advantage of it.

It seems clear however that the sources are addressing different situations. On every level there are some sins which a person still feels as sins, while there are others to which all sensitivity has been lost. As regards the first, failure to make any move towards repentance is considered a grave sin. On the other hand, if one's repentance reaches even those sins for which feeling has been lost, this is considered a free-will offering and Hashem is "grateful" to him.

THE WORLD OF TRUTH

In another Gemara we read:

> In the future Hashem will bring the *yetzer ha-ra'* and slaughter it in front of the *tsaddikim* and *resha'im*. To the former it seems like a high mountain; to the latter, like a thread of hair. Each group weeps. The *tsaddikim* weep [saying]: How were we ever able to conquer such a high mountain! The *resha'im* weep [saying]: How were we not able to conquer such a thread of hair![5]

The meaning is as we have explained above. The higher a person rises in spiritual level, the harder his service becomes: "The greater the person, the greater his *yetzer*."[6] It is said that on the highest levels, the service of God becomes unimaginably difficult.

But at the early stages it is relatively easy. In "the

world of truth" pictured in the Gemara, there are no exaggerations and no "literary flourishes." If the Gemara says they both weep, we can take it that this is neither more nor less than the truth. The *tsaddikim* weep with joy at the tremendous privilege granted them by Hashem to overcome the fearful power of the *yetzer ha-ra'* at those high levels. The wicked weep at their own foolishness: why did they not *begin*? Beginnings are relatively easy; why did they not conquer that thread of hair?

Whenever thoughts of despair enter a person's mind, such as, "I see I never succeed; I cannot do any better," etc., he should know that this is nonsense. Why should he despair? He has not started yet; he is still standing before the thread of hair. If anyone should despair, it is the *tsaddik* who faces the mighty mountain of high-level service. But the fact is that *he* does not despair; he battles on and eventually conquers the mighty mountain.

□□□□□□□

If we will but begin, we shall, with God's help, succeed.   □

notes

1 *Yoma* 86a.
2 *Hoshea'* 14:5.
3 *Netivot 'Olam, Netiv Ha-teshuva*, ch. 3.
4 *Sha'arei Teshuva* 1:2.
5 *Sukka* 52b.
6 Ibid.

How one who is far off
should learn *mussar*

□□□

What can we do? We see without the slightest doubt that we are not stirred by our *mussar* learning. But maybe we have not grasped how *mussar* should be learned.

We possess a conscious mind and a subconscious mind. The subconscious mind is amenable to training, like some animals. If one gives clear and repeated commands, it will obey. For example, it will obey instructions to wake up at a certain time.

The subconscious reacts to hypnotic stimuli. In an experiment, someone under hypnosis was told to sign his name after 3,000 minutes. He woke up from his trance and, although he was not at all good at arithmetic, as soon as the precise number of minutes elapsed he took a piece of paper and signed his name on it, without being able to explain why he did it. This demonstrates the extent to which the subconscious is amenable to instructions.

Desires and volitions are also located in the subconscious, from which they emerge to exert influence on the conscious mind. The conscious, thinking mind then incorporates these influences into its system and becomes biased, refusing to accept ideas or conclusions that oppose the desires.

INFLUENCING THE SUBCONSCIOUS

How to exert influence on the subconscious? This may be done in various ways. One of the most effective is the use of the imagination. Thoughts and logical arguments may have difficulty in penetrating the subconscious, but images can reach down and affect the subconscious springs of action.

When the masters of *mussar* said that one has to bring the message down to the physical level, they meant that it has to reach the subconscious mind. This is not so difficult. The method they adopted was to produce vivid images of the Day of Judgment, through which they succeeded in engendering fear of Divine justice. This was extremely effective in keeping one's actions under control.

My saintly great-grandfather, Rabbi Yisrael Salanter *z.ts.l.*, indicated a source for this in the Gemara,[1] which records a story of a certain *ḥassid* (referring to the great *tanna* Rabbi Yehuda b. R. Ila'i) whose wife annoyed him on the eve of Rosh Hashana, whereupon he decided to spend the night in the local cemetery. Rabbi Yisrael explains that he did this in order to help him engender images of the day of death, which would restrain his anger.

Rabbi Menaḥem Recanati, in a wonderful passage in his commentary on the Torah,[2] has this to say on the mystical function of offerings:

> An offering brings the lower will near [to the higher spheres] and unifies it and brings it into association

with the higher will; and at the same time it brings the higher will into association with the lower will, uniting it with the latter.

Here, in mystical language, is the essence of what we have been discussing. The "higher will" is the spiritual enlightenment which reaches the heart [the subconscious] by way of the intellect, in accordance with the verse, "You shall know today [in the conscious mind], and return it into your heart [into the subconscious]."[3] The "lower will" is the natural, instinctive will of man's lower nature, centered in the subconscious. The offering unites them; it brings the lower into contact with the higher, and vice versa. How does it achieve this?

ACT OF IMAGINATION

Rabbi Recanati continues:

> He who brings an offering binds his soul to the soul of the offering, and it is counted to him as if he had sacrificed his own soul.

It is clear that what we are talking about here is *an act of imagination*. By making the offering, a vivid picture of sacrifice is presented to the lower self. This becomes fixed in the subconscious, which thus becomes more amenable to the suggestions of the higher will. The higher will has in a sense been "brought down" to the lower. Eventually, there are prospects that the subconscious will be led to accept the conscious, intellectual will as its own; it will have been "raised to" and "unified with" the higher level.

TECHNIQUE OF *MUSSAR*

My great-grandfather Rabbi Yisrael Salanter adds in one of his letters that it is a good idea, when learning *mussar*, to repeat the same statement many times. The fact is that this method is very effective in influencing the subconscious, which, animal-like, is amenable to training by repetition. It is a well-known fact, as we said earlier, that if a person wants to wake up at a certain time he only has to issue repeated commands to his subconscious and these will be obeyed, even if no reason is given for the order. The subconscious acts instinctively, without need for rationale.

It follows that if one thinks over and over again of the disgrace involved in arrogance, avarice, failure to learn Torah, failure to pray properly — even without introducing any novel ideas — one will find that this has a great effect. Simple repetition, whether in thoughts or in words, can affect the springs of action.

□□□□□□□

The main point is that our lack of will to learn *mussar* or to spend any time at all in serious reflection is a direct result of the rise of the lower will from the subconscious to the conscious mind. We have explained elsewhere[4] that the essential *timtum ha-lev* ("blockage of the heart") is the will not to reflect. □

notes

1 *Berachot* 18b.
2 *Parashat Noaḥ*, folio 39d.
3 *Devarim* 4:39.
4 See p. 67.

The Day of Atonement

God is the mikveh *of Yisrael*

> Rabbi Akiva said: Happy are you, Yisrael! Before
> whom do you purify yourselves and who purifies you?
> Your Father in heaven…"God is the *mikveh* of Yis-
> rael":[1] just as a *mikveh* purifies the defiled, so the Holy
> One, blessed be He, purifies Yisrael.[2]

The idea of immersion in a *mikveh* is that one, so to
speak, goes out of the world of falsehood, goes out of
this world completely; even one's hair must remain
within the *mikveh*. As we know, "water" stands for
"the water of knowledge,"[3] that is, the Torah. Total
immersion in the *mikveh* means total immersion in
Torah. And more: one's contact with Torah must be
complete; nothing at all may intervene between oneself
and the Torah. The Torah into which he enters must be
purely spiritual, without any worldly thoughts whatsoever. "Drawn water" disqualifies a *mikveh* because
such water has been contained in a vessel used for
worldly purposes. The vessel disqualifies the water

even though it was drawn expressly for a *mikveh*, for the purpose of purification. If the *mikveh* contains insufficient water, the drawn water may even disqualify the whole *mikveh*. Even if there is sufficient water in the *mikveh*, it is disqualified if the water is seeping out (*zoḥalin*). The fact that it is on the decrease is sufficient as a disqualifying factor. Only one type of *mikveh* remains fit for use even if water is flowing out of it, and that is a *mikveh* fed by spring water, which constantly renews itself from its source. If the water reaches the *mikveh* by way of an object which is susceptible to *tum'ah*, this can also disqualify the *mikveh*. Any contact with even the possibility of defilement is sufficient to prevent the purification from taking effect. From these laws of immersion one can learn something about the conditions of complete attachment to Torah.

Hashem is in fact a pool of purification for the people of Israel, provided that they are completely attached to Him, recognizing in their hearts that there is no one but He. On *Yom Kippur* the *yetzer ha-ra'* has less power, and consequently, attachment to Hashem can be more intense. In a sense therefore, Israel "immerses itself in God" — a very remarkable thought.

2 □□□

"a bribe to Satan*"*

In some of our sources we come across the difficult concept of "giving a bribe" to *Satan*, the accusing angel, in order to "buy him off," so to speak. Ramban, in his commentary on *Vayikra*, associates this concept with the goat which is sent into the desert, "to 'Azazel," on the Day of Atonement (*Vayikra* 16:8).

In an earlier article on "Obstinacy"[4] we explained the nature of this deplorable character trait. We compared it to the action of a coiled spring, which shows more resistance the more one presses down on it. In spiritual life, too, one sometimes finds that the more one demonstrates a truth to someone, the more obstinately he resists it. In that section, some of the dire consequences of this *midda* were described.

In view of this danger, it is usually advisable to pursue one's ongoing war with the *yetzer ha-ra'* by cunning and subterfuge, avoiding a head-on collision as much as possible. A head-on clash with the *yetzer* would only activate the "spring syndrome" and increase its resistance to unmanageable proportions. A tactic which often proves successful in such cases is to satisfy the trait of obstinacy by making some small "concession" giving the impression that the *yetzer* has won the day. If the intention is absolutely sincere, it may be possible in this way to trick the *yetzer* into withdrawing its usual resistance to the good one wishes to do. This is what is called "a bribe to *Satan*."

The Torah commands us to "send a goat to 'Azazel" as part of the service of the Day of Atonement in the Holy Temple.[5] This goat must be exactly similar in appearance, height and value, to its companion, the goat whose blood is sprinkled before the Ark in the Holy of Holies on this most sacred day.[6] It is chosen by lot, proclaimed as "for 'Azazel" and taken to that rocky place in the desert, giving the appearance of being, God forbid, a sacrifice to the demons of the wilderness. But in fact, of course, it is like its companion, a sacrifice to Hashem. By sending it out into the desert we are fulfilling the command of Hashem. Ramban, in his commentary,[7] emphasizes that all the actions associated with the goat are completely *l'shem shamayim*. The fact that it atones for our sins establishes, beyond the slightest doubt, that it belongs solely to the realm of *kedusha*. Why then the appearance of a sacrifice to the Other Side? The answer is — to soften our obstinacy by deceiving the Other Side into thinking we have made a "concession." The *yetzer ha-ra'*, which is so fond of deceiving others, is itself easily deceived.

This is what is meant by the "bribe to *Satan*." When *Satan* thinks his will is being followed, he will no longer disturb us as insistently with his incitements. This resembles the well-known tactic of "putting off" the *yetzer ha-ra'* by telling him that we agree in principle, but it is not convenient at the moment. By these means one can succeed in evading him entirely.

It is customary to tie the *parshiyot* of the *tefillin* with the hairs of a cow and to let some of the hair show on the outside. This is "to show the 'accusers' that they too have a share in the mitzva...."[8] The "hair of the cow" alludes, of course, to the sin of the making of the Golden Calf, and the idea is similar to the above — to ameliorate stubbornness by making a gesture in the direction of the *yetzer ha-ra'*.

CURIOSITY

The Gemara remarks that the Torah forbids nothing without allowing something similar. "It forbids a married woman but permits a divorcee; it forbids a sister-in-law but permits levirate marriage; it forbids pork but permits a fish called *shibuta* whose brain has a similar taste; it forbids a mixture of meat and milk and permits the udder of the cow."⁹ The idea behind this is that the Torah wishes to undermine that insatiable curiosity which insists on tasting everything and enjoying everything.¹⁰ By allowing a person to "taste" the *issur* in a permitted way, the sting is taken out of the curiosity, in the same way that obstinacy is mitigated as described before.

But one must remember that the little concessions, if they are to achieve the desired result, must be made solely for the purest of motives. If they are made because of weakness or laziness, they will have the opposite effect to that intended. Even if we are talking about permitted pleasures, Ramban has taught us that it is possible to be "a scoundrel licensed by the Torah."¹¹ If we wish to obtain maximum aid for our spiritual progress, we must fight against laxities of this sort as much as we possibly can.

We must put maximum effort into Torah learning, both in depth and in diligence, in all sincerity. We must also make an effort to have a fixed time each day for *mussar* reflection *in the truth perspective.*¹² Then we shall begin to see in our hearts the light of a truth that we have not hitherto perceived, and to hear within us truths not previously audible. With effort and self-arousal we merit heavenly aid, and with the perspective of truth we merit redemption.

3 □□□

between man and his fellow

We have explained earlier that *Yom Kippur* means that
a person is, so to speak, transported temporarily out of
this world and that he attaches himself to Hashem
alone. By being attached to the Source, he is able to
bring about that "Divine Return" we have referred to
in a previous article.[13]

This attachment can be achieved only while in a state
of *unity*. Just as God is one, so must the person who
attaches himself to Him be one in inner unity — to be
completely united, as the verse says, "And Israel (*singular*) encamped" at Sinai — "with one heart,"[14] at
peace with one another. If one feels in discord with his
neighbor, this means that one's ego is in the fore, and in
this state one can hardly establish close contact with
Hashem.

SINS BETWEEN MAN AND MAN

It is well known that sins between man and his neighbor are not atoned for by *Yom Kippur*, unless forgiveness is first obtained from the person who has been
sinned against.[15] A kabbalistic reason for this is given
by Rabbi M. Cordovero[16] in these terms:

> The souls appear before God on this day by mystical
> association with the Root of all souls. Those souls who
> subdue themselves in *teshuva* arouse the Divine
> Return...but if there is discord between them...there
> is division in the higher Root...the light of *teshuva*
> cannot shine on one who creates discord and division in

that very light…The mystical number of souls is six-hundred thousand…and if the supernal light is to be attracted, six-hundred thousand "with one heart" are required. There can be unity with the great and holy Name only when they too are in complete unity….

Rabbi Cordovero does not confine his remarks to sins between man and his fellow. It is not simply that sins of this nature cannot be atoned for on *Yom Kippur* without obtaining one's neighbor's forgiveness, because, failing this, the sin is not corrected. It appears that he maintains that while there is still disunity, *Yom Kippur* cannot atone for *any* of one's sins. This can only be because disunity contradicts the very essence of *Yom Kippur*.

4 ☐☐

Yom Kippur: *extension of its light throughout the year*

Our Rabbis have said that an individual is given a special chance to do *teshuva* during the Ten Days of Penitence; they apply to him the verse "Seek Hashem when He may be found."[17]

What can an individual do after *Yom Kippur* is over? It is possible to extend the light of *Yom Kippur* to illuminate one's heart during the whole year. The self-arousal that affected him on *Yom Kippur* should not be forgotten; he should reflect on it and use it afterwards too. He should constantly renew the resolutions he made on *Yom Kippur*. To the extent that *Yom Kippur* stays alive within him, to that same extent he will progress and prosper spiritually. R. Simḥa Zissel advised us to bear in mind constantly the thoughts and feelings experienced during the most intense moments of *Yom Kippur*. Once these memories are dimmed, *Yom Kippur* has slipped away and the whole process of forgiveness is in question.

Just as the Gemara indicates in the case of the rainfall allocated to a particular community, which may vary not only in amount, but also in time and place,[18] so also the "instruments" given to an individual may be very finely adjusted in accordance with his precise spiritual level. A person's happiness in this world depends on the way he uses the instruments he is given. If he uses what he has for spiritual advancement, he will find that he reaches satisfaction in a physical sense, too: "You will eat and be satisfied."[19] If not, satisfaction will remain forever beyond his reach: "No man dies with half his desires attained."[20]

Similarly, if suffering is his lot and he uses his suffering for spiritual advancement, he will find comfort in this. Suffering may be terribly hard to bear, but when he realizes that it has helped him in all eternity, he may even come to appreciate it. (My *rebbe* gave a wonderful illustration of this. If a person were ordered to spend his days in taking off people's shoes and putting them on again, he would feel this as a burden and a disgrace. But if he happens to own a shoe shop stocked with a very popular line of shoes, and his shop is full of customers asking him to measure their feet for shoe-size hundreds of times a day, he will be only too happy to comply. But what has happened to the disgrace and the burden? It is clear that all this is relative to the advantage gained.)

To sum up: To the extent that we succeed in taking the impressions of the Days of Awe with us into the year, so shall we prosper and make progress and be happy throughout the year, in our physical lives, and certainly in a spiritual sense, for all eternity in the World to Come.

5 □□

the essence of the day atones

It is the stated opinion of Rabbi Yehuda Ha-Nasi (known as "Rabbi") that *Yom Kippur* effects atonement even without repentance, because "the essence of the day atones."[21] The principle involved here needs elucidation. Even according to the accepted *halacha* that *Yom Kippur* is effective only with repentance on our part, there are some forms of atonement which do not require repentance. Rambam writes: "The goat which is sent out atones for all sins...provided that the person has done *teshuva*. Without *teshuva* it atones only for the lighter sins...that is, for negative and positive commands not involving the penalty of *karet*."[22] Rambam also mentions the concept of "the essence of the day," although (as Rabbi Karo points out in *Kesef Mishneh*) this can apply only after one has repented, since we do not accept the view of Rabbi.

We have to understand the whole concept of atonement without *teshuva*. Surely this would be like immersing in a *mikveh* with the source of *tum'ah* still in one's hands? And if one has done *teshuva*, what does the "essence of the day" contribute to the atonement?

I have heard in the name of Rabbi Yitzḥak Blaser (one of the most outstanding disciples of Rabbi Yisrael Salanter) that a person can easily find out whether he has succeeded in obtaining Divine forgiveness on *Yom Kippur*. Our Rabbis say that sin obstructs the heart.[23] Therefore if the sin has been removed, the obstruction must also have been removed. It follows that if after *Yom Kippur* a person feels his heart is pure and obstruction-free, this is a sure sign that his sins have been forgiven. If, however, his heart is in the same state as before, as obstructed and obtuse as ever, it is clear that his sins have not been forgiven.

If this is so, Rabbi's view is even more difficult to understand. If the day "effects atonement without the need for repentance," every Jew, after *Yom Kippur*, should feel that same purity of heart described by Rabbi Blaser, even if he has not so much as thought of repentance. But we know very well that this is not so!

On the other hand, we find that the early Ḥassidic masters used to teach their followers (even the simplest) to rejoice and dance at the outgoing of *Yom Kippur*, from the joy of having one's sins atoned. But what point would there be in rejoicing over atonement if the heart's obstruction is still felt? Surely this shows that the sins are still there?

OPENING THE GATE

The truth is that there are many different levels of repentance, and correspondingly, many different levels of forgiveness. Rabbenu Yona has taught us that "every repentance finds some forgiveness...but only complete repentance purifies the soul...to gain complete forgiveness."[24] If a person succeeds in uprooting and defeating the *yetzer ha-ra'*, then the consequent atonement results in the dissolution of the heart's obstruction. But sometimes the *yetzer* is only "put to sleep." In that case the obstruction, though still very much alive, may also be temporarily incapacitated.

The "essence of the day" of *Yom Kippur* is unique in that Hashem has put it out of bounds for the power of evil. Not that the *yetzer ha-ra'* has been destroyed; its activities merely have been restricted. It has been "put to sleep." The "stone on the heart" has less power. The gate is open; repentance is that much easier. If at the outgoing of *Yom Kippur* a person throws himself anew into holy service, the obstruction will not reawaken. It will gradually disappear.

The "essence of the day" thus effects only a beginning. The person's own arousal completes the process. This beginning is the atonement referred to by Rabbi. The other Sages agree that the day itself has some power. It helps, with repentance (or the sending of the goat to 'Azazel, as mentioned by Rambam), to achieve full atonement. But on its own, the day is powerless.

CASTING OFF THE YOKE

So everything depends on the outgoing of *Yom Kippur*. Everyone agrees that on *Yom Kippur* the power of the *yetzer* is restricted. As is well known, *Satan* has no power to make accusations against Israel on that day.[25] (As we have mentioned elsewhere,[26] the *Satan*'s "accusation" is only another aspect of the *yetzer's* "seduction.") When *Yom Kippur* goes out, if one awakens the *yetzer* it will return with redoubled force, as if *Yom Kippur* had never been.

As soon as the fast is over, most people throw off with relief the yoke of *Yom Kippur* and its thoughts; and if the truth be told, the yoke of its resolutions, too. This is what Rabbi Blaser meant when he said the "obstruction" remains in place. It may not have been so noticeable on *Yom Kippur* itself, but it soon revives, and nothing of *Yom Kippur* is left. The sins are all there, just as they were previously. The custom of dancing at the conclusion of the fast may be not so much to celebrate the disappearance of one's sins as to help bring about their disappearance. Such atonement as has been achieved on *Yom Kippur* may thereby be extended and given permanence.

But it is important to be sure that the motives for the joy are pure. When dancing, it is only too easy for the joy to degenerate into a feeling of relief that the days of penitence are over.

□□□□□□□

To sum up: The atonement of *Yom Kippur* proves itself only after *Yom Kippur*. There is great danger that one might slacken one's efforts. May Hashem help us to maintain our spiritual strength!

6 □□

extension to Sukkot, Shemini Atzeret *and* Simḥat Torah

We begin preparing for *Sukkot* immediately after *Yom Kippur*, so that the spirit of *Yom Kippur* can be caught up in the festival. From *Yom Kippur* we bring an awakening of repentance, resolutions for change, aspirations for spiritual growth. Or anyway, that is what we ought to bring from it. On *Yom Kippur* there is no *yetzer ha-ra'*, but it tends to revive afterwards. How can we retain the spirit of *Yom Kippur* after *Yom Kippur* is over?

Conservation — that is the way. The essence of the *sukka* lies in conservation or preservation. (We express this in the *Hashkivenu* prayer: "Spread over us the *sukka* of Your peace ... and protect us in the shadow of Your wings.") The kabbalists say that the *sukka* is a kind of "Noaḥ's ark," again giving us the idea of protection from the threatening forces of destruction. One who sits in the *sukka* and deliberately sets out to engender thoughts and feelings of Torah and *yir'at shamayim*, and to exclude thoughts of the *yetzer ha-ra'*, will inevitably feel something of the protective power of the mitzva of *sukka*. He will — at least to some extent — have the feeling that the "gates are shut against defilement."

When the Rabbis said that the mitzva of dwelling in the *sukka* involves living in the *sukka* in precisely the same way as one normally lives in a house,[27] they meant that we should bring all our normal, physical activities under the influence of the *sukka*. The *sukka* creates a very special atmosphere which can convert ordinary, physical activities into spiritually motivated acts. Indeed, one must not eat outside the *sukka* for that very reason.

The Four Species, which are also a mitzva unique to *Sukkot*, contain the secret of attachment to Hashem and the removal of all disturbing influences, symbolized by the "bad winds and bad dews" mentioned in the Gemara.[28] Taking the Four Species also exemplifies the preservative effect of *Sukkot*. In a positive sense, they bring a spirit of holiness to arouse and reinforce the holy spark within every Jewish heart.

The joy which is a special characteristic of *Sukkot* is a function of all these far-reaching spiritual effects. Even more, the joy itself produces completely new effects — it produces the Holy Spirit. "Why was the ceremony of the water-drawing called *Simḥat Bet Ha-sho'evah* ("the Joy of the Water-drawing") — because thence they would draw the Holy Spirit."[29] "Thence," that is, from the joy itself; joy is the source of the Holy Spirit.[30]

These are all ways in which a person is helped to maintain his position and introduce the spirit of *Yom Kippur* to the whole year. *Sukkot* is referred to as "seven days in the year"[31] — seven days which influence the whole year.[32]

A CHANCE FOR THE NATIONS

In the Messianic era, when the nations of the world will ask for another chance, God will test them by the mitzva of *sukka*.[33] Why just *sukka*? Because whatever degree of *teshuva* they attain needs a *sukka* to preserve it.

The seventy bulls offered as part of the *mussafim* during the first seven days of *Sukkot* are to atone for the seventy nations of the world.[34] They, too, will eventually receive enlightenment from Hashem, for the world is not set to rights until the whole of creation sees the truth. There can be no exceptions; as we say in the prayers of the *yamim ha-noraim*: "Let Your fear rest upon all Your works." Only then can it be said that "You will reign, O God, alone...."

□□□□□□□

The seventh and last day of *Sukkot* is *Hoshana Rabba*, on which, we are told, the final verdicts are handed down for delivery to their various destinations.[35] This means that the final verdict is reached only when it is seen how Israel has used the opportunities afforded by the *sukka* and the *lulav* to preserve the spirit of *Yom Kippur* and introduce it into the entire year. It is then that the person's individual level is fixed, and this itself is the final verdict. □

notes

1 *Yirmiya* 17:13.
2 *Yoma* 85b.
3 Rambam, *Mishneh Torah, Hilchot Mikva'ot* 11:12.
4 See p. 68.
5 *Vayikra* 16:10.

6 Ibid. 16:15.
7 On *Vayikra* 16:8.
8 Radvaz, *Ta'amei Ha-mitzvot*, no. 79.
9 *Ḥullin* 109a.
10 See Volume II, p.105.
11 On *Vayikra* 19:2.
12 See Volume I, pp. 161 et seq.
13 See p. 90.
14 *Shemot* 19:2, Rashi.
15 *Yoma* 85b.
16 *'Avodat Ha-kodesh*, no. 16.
17 *Rosh Hashana* 18a.
18 Ibid. 17b.
19 *Devarim* 11:15.
20 *Yesha'ya* 55:6. See *Rosh Hashana* 18a.
21 *Yoma* 85b.
22 *Hilchot Teshuva* 1:2.
23 *Yoma* 39a.
24 *Sha'arei Teshuva* 1:9.
25 *Yoma* 20a.
26 See p. 24.
27 *Sukka* 28b.
28 Ibid. 37b.
29 *Yerushalmi, Sukka* 5:1.
30 *Sefat Emet* V, p. 182.
31 *Vayikra* 23:41.
32 *Sefat Emet* V, p. 200.
33 *'Avoda Zara* 3a.
34 *Sukka* 55b.
35 Zohar II 142a; III 32a.

Nature

□□□□□□□□□□□□□□□□□□□□□□□□□□□□□□□□□□□□□□□

The first lecture in this series was given in Gateshead in 1944. The year is significant, and one cannot avoid the impression that the many references to the Generation of the Deluge have a bearing on the deluge of destruction which was then engulfing world Jewry.

This article is a classic example of Rabbi Dessler's methodology, based on that of Maharal, by which the most recondite and difficult *aggadot* and *midrashim* can be made to yield important and relevant insights.

The "materialism" of the title is not the theoretical materialism of the lecture hall, but the practical materialism which gives precedence to material concerns over the spiritual concerns on which the future of mankind depends. The basic idea of this article is already contained in "The Wisdom of the World," Volume I, pp. 195-202.

The destructive philosophy of materialism

□□□

Human beings believe, in their arrogance, that if they continue developing the world on the basis of an ever-expanding science and technology, they will eventually achieve an environment that will afford everyone unlimited gratification of the senses and a life of untrammeled ease and pleasure.

There can be no greater error than this. Material progress is a double-edged sword. Advancement in one direction is more than offset by deterioration in another. The great benefits of civilization are invariably accompanied by its degradations. People don't want to understand that uncorrected human nature will ruin all their efforts. If people become "givers,"[1] the world will be a wonderful place to live in, irrespective of technology. So long as they remain "takers," their efforts will inevitably be directed toward selfishness, violence and war. Every advance in technology will be used for destruction and ruin. For instance, the vast improvement in transport which we have witnessed in our time, the ability to reach any place on the globe within hours or days rather than weeks or months — what a benefit for those who are bent on doing mitzvot! But on the other hand, what a danger it poses to humanity! Previously wars were localized, but now any war is likely to become a world conflict. With great perception our Rabbis said: "Ease of assembly — if for *tsaddikim* — is good for them and good for the world; if for *resha'im* — it is bad for them and bad for the world."[2]

Every new advance, every invention, is good — provided it is used by *tsaddikim*. How does one become a *tsaddik*? Here the world makes its biggest error. It believes that human nature will "somehow" perfect itself — a mistake that even the greatest fool should be ashamed of.

Only when *Mashiah* comes and "the world will be full of the knowledge of God like the waters cover the sea bed,"[3] — that is, when all will at last become "givers" instead of "takers" — only then will there be a perfected world.

This is the profound truth enshrined in the Targum to *Yesha'ya* 62:1:[4]

> Until I bring salvation to Zion
> I shall grant no rest to the nations;
> Until I bring comfort to Yerushalayim
> I shall allow no peace to the kingdoms;
> Until her light shines forth like the dawn
> And her salvation like a burning flame.

ADVANCED TECHNOLOGY

The Torah clearly indicates its outlook on technological advances made by and for the *resha'im*. When recounting the achievements of the descendants of Cain, it lists "Tuval-Cain, sharpener of all implements of bronze and iron." If this refers to the advent of the Iron Age, we could certainly hail it as a great turning point in human civilization. Previously man had to till his soil with implements of wood and stone, and now Tuval-Cain succeeded in providing mankind with easily sharpened metal instruments. What a difference in food production and in lightening the labor load! But our Rabbis explain it rather differently. They tell us that the Torah saw in this the seeds of destruction. They comment:

> What is the meaning of "Tuval-Cain"? It means that he added spice to the profession of Cain (*tuval* from *tavlin*, "spices"); he improved the tools of Cain's profession, provided better weapons for murderers.[5]

And again, in the instructions regarding altar stones, we find that the Torah disqualifies any stone that is hewn or even touched by any iron implement. "If you have raised your sword over it, you have defiled it."[6] But why should all iron tools be called swords? Ramban, in his commentary on this verse, brings examples to show that all implements with sharp cutting edges are called *ḥerev* (sword) in Hebrew. But this, too, needs explanation. Why should *all* sharp tools bear the stigma of destruction? The answer can only lie in what we stated above — before the world is perfected people will inevitably use all their potential for evil.

(Rashi on the same verse, quoting from the *Mechilta*, states that it is not right that the altar, which was created to lengthen people's lives, should be shaped by iron, which was created to shorten people's lives. The last phrase seems difficult until we realize that it refers to the unredeemed world which was created defective in many respects, and which needs human input to give it positive content. When the Rabbis said that without the Torah the world would revert to chaos,[7] they meant that the chaotic nature of unredeemed man would bring about its destruction; it can be saved only by the injection of holiness from redeemed man.)

WATERS OF EDEN

The same idea can be derived from the *Midrash Ha-ne'elam*:[8] "There is water that nurtures the wise, and there is water that nurtures fools. The water that nurtures the wise is from those drops which derive from Eden..."[9] "Eden" symbolizes the holy soul of man; the "water that nurtures the wise" is the water of Torah, which nurtures the spiritually wise. The "water that nurtures fools" is the underground water of the *tehom*, the bottomless abyss, which represents the materialistic philosophy of the world, changing nothing in man's essential being. Whoever uses wisdom and science merely to expand man's physical capabilities increases stupidity and destructiveness in the world. We refer once again to that famous passage in the *Duties of the Heart*, part of which we have already quoted elsewhere:[10]

> Their evil inclination induces them to abandon the [spiritual] world wherein lies their salvation...it makes self-adornment more attractive to them [than inner goodness]...it impels them to gratify their desires for self-indulgence...until they are sunk in the depths of its seas; and the evil inclination obliges them to undergo the pain and distress of those fierce waves... and *the more their world is established the more their mind is ruined.*

Now we turn to a very interesting Gemara[11] which recounts in figurative terms what happened when David was digging the foundations of the Temple.[12]

> When David was digging the *shittin* (conduits in the rock through which the sacred libations flowed to the *tehom* below[13]) the *tehom* rose and threatened to flood the world.

Rashi records in the name of the *Talmud Yerushalmi* how the *tehom* rose. He writes that David came upon a potsherd which raised its voice and said, "Don't take me away from here; I am wedged here against the *tehom* from the day the Torah was given and the whole earth trembled." But David refused to listen and removed it.

The meaning of the parable is that with the giving of the Torah, Hashem raised a secure barrier against materialism and its philosophy, which is symbolized by "the waters of *tehom*." David wanted the holiness symbolized by the wine and water libations in the Holy Temple to penetrate the *tehom* and redeem the materialism that they represent, and therefore he wanted to deepen the conduits as much as possible. Yet...

> ...the *tehom* rose and threatened to flood the world.

Once access to the *tehom* had been given, it ran out of control.

> ...[David] wrote the Divine Name on a sherd and threw it into the *tehom*, which then descended and remained in its place.

There was no other alternative but to introduce a "Holy Name" — high-powered spirituality — to stem the advance. Even then the Holy Name was erased; great and lofty concepts which have it in their power to prevent the spread of materialism nevertheless suffer in the process. This may give us some idea of the danger to which those who enter the realm of materialistic philosophy are exposed.

The Gemara[14] concludes the story by adding that there was an overreaction.

> The *tehom* descended 16,000 *amot*. When he saw it had descended too far, he [David] said, 'The higher it is, the moister the earth is.' He recited the fifteen Songs of Degrees[15] and brought it up 15,000 *amot*, keeping it at a depth of 1,000 *amot*.

The meaning is that if the *tehom* of materialism is driven too far from human consciousness, free will is impaired. The symbolism of the fifteen Songs of Degrees is related to the fifteen steps of the *Dayenu* liturgy in the Haggadah, corresponding, according to the Vilna Gaon, to the earth and the seven heavens with the seven intervening spaces, which all refer to steps in the internal purifying process of the human heart.[16]

RAINFALL AND THE FLOOD

The *tehom* is also involved in the incomparable blessing of rainfall. The Midrash tells us:

> Rabbi Shimon ben Elazar says: No handsbreadth of rain descends from above without the *tehom* rising two handsbreadths to meet it... Rabbi Levi said: The upper waters are "masculine" and the lower waters "feminine," and the former say to the latter: Accept us;

you are creatures of the Almighty and we are His
ambassadors. Straightaway they accept them.[17]

At the commencement of the Flood we find the same
idea:

> On the seventeenth [of the month] the waters of the
> Flood descended from Heaven. They were "mascu-
> line" waters. And the waters of the *tehom*, which are
> "feminine" waters, rose [to meet them]. They joined
> together to overwhelm and destroy the world.[18]

The Flood started as beneficial rainfall, as Rashi comments on the verse, "The rainfall came upon the
earth."[19] "He caused the rain to descend at first with
mercy; if the people would repent, it would remain a
rainfall of blessing. Only when they did not repent, did
it turn into a deluge."

The "rainfall which comes from above" represents
the flow of material blessings which Hashem sends us
in response to our mitzvot. "He who learns Torah in
spite of poverty will be given the means to learn it in
affluence."[20] We have often quoted the words of Rambam who explains the promise: "If you listen to My
voice...I will give the rainfall of your land in its proper
time" as assuring us that if we keep God's mitzvot well,
we shall be given the means to keep them still better.[21]
Even the greatly expanded blessings of *Parashat Behu-
kotai*[22] — "threshing time will overtake the grape har-
vest," etc. — have the same function. This redeems the
material world by making it solely a vehicle for the
service of Hashem.

This is what is meant by "material blessings which
come from holiness." They "come from" holiness in
the sense that this is their ultimate purpose. Therefore

"rains of blessing" come "from above," i.e., from the infinite love of Hashem; and they are "received by" the waters of the *tehom*, which "rise up to meet them," meaning that the physical senses feel the holiness of God's love and are refined and sanctified by it. [This is the meaning of "masculine waters" and "feminine waters." The "masculine waters" refer to the Divine input, the "feminine waters" to the human response.]

TWO PARALLEL WORLDS

But there is also an influx of this-worldly affluence coming from the direction of defilement. Again, "coming from" must be taken in the sense of "ultimate purpose." Is there anything whose *purpose* is defilement? Yes. Everything in the spiritual realm is mirrored by something in the material realm. "God made [two worlds] one corresponding to the other."[23] There is a type of affluence which is given to the *rasha'* in this world and whose purpose is to provide a challenge and a temptation to other people. It enables the *Satan* to persuade shortsighted people that being a *rasha'* is "worthwhile."[24] But in the long run, this type of influx is self-destructive. When "the measure is filled," the wicked are destroyed.

This type of influx begins "from below," i.e., from the materialistic side. Divine love comes to meet it from above [since God does not willingly abandon any of His creatures]; but when the two influences mingle, and it is apparent that the *resha'im* continue in their rebellion and refuse to repent, the very mercy of God turns into strict severity. "*Resha'im* succeed in changing God's mercy into severity."[25] The reason is that severity then becomes the most merciful course. The enforced submission of the *rasha'* to God's justice is the best possible fate for the *rasha'* himself. Even his ultimate destruction is an atonement. The destructive mingling of the influx from above and the influx from below symbolizes the conversion of God's very mercy into strict justice. In such extreme cases *God's love takes on the guise of the most severe and implacable justice*, as exemplified by the Deluge itself. It is significant that in the case of the Deluge "the fountains of the great deep" (the underground waters of the *tehom*) invade the earth first, and only later are "the windows of heaven opened."[26]

The Targum Yonatan on this last quoted verse sheds a bizarre light on the last moments of the world before the Deluge:

> The foundations of the great deep were broken asunder, and the sons of men placed their children there to block up the cracks with their bodies, and only then were the windows of heaven opened.

We find a similar idea in the *midrash*:[27]

> "The mercies of the wicked are cruel":[28] This refers to the generation of the Flood, who were cruel...When the Almighty brought the deeps upon them...they took their children and placed them over the *tehom* and pressed down upon them.

And another *midrash*[29] is a little more explicit:

> They had many children and each one took his son and placed him over the *tehom* and pressed down upon him, to patch up the damage, so that the water should not overwhelm them. And when the waters became too

strong, they took their other children and did the same
again. Look at their mercy! Truly, "the mercies of the
wicked are cruel."

What can be the meaning of this extraordinary *midrash*? The fact is that the more men pursue the goal of
developing the world materialistically, the more their
troubles increase. Instead of realizing that they are
sinking further and further into the mire of materialism, they search for ever more sophisticated technological devices, hoping that by these means they will
eventually reach their coveted goal — a life of physical
ease and happiness in *this* world, without having to
bother about the demands and challenges of the spiritual world. And when they see no hope of this for
themselves, they make desperate efforts to ensure that
at least their children will be able to enjoy material
happiness in this world. It is really amazing to see how
blind people are. How can they fail to see that all their
efforts backfire, that all the research of all their learned
economists cannot keep their economy on an even keel!
Yet they persist in thinking that soon, very soon, they
will hit the right formula, and if not in this generation,
then in the next universal happiness will surely come.
And so they bring up their children to study nothing
and think of nothing but technological advancement
and, figuratively speaking, they try to forestall with
their childrens' bodies the inevitable collapse of the
materialistic civilization. They don't want to know
that their children, too, will not be saved.

However much they try to patch over the cracks,
there is no salvation from the ultimate collapse of the
world of defilement. The "mercy" they extend to their

children by continuing to educate them in this way is in reality nothing but cruelty. They are only ensuring their destruction.

☐☐☐☐☐☐☐

The only way to a happy life in this world is the way of Torah: being satisfied with a minimum of worldly things while having a great ambition for things spiritual. As our Rabbis said: "This is the way of Torah: eat bread and salt...and labor in the Torah...Happy are you in *this* world!"[30] ☐

notes

1 See Volume I, p. 119.
2 *Sanhedrin* 71a.
3 *Yesha'ya* 11:9 (*Metzudat David*).
4 See Volume I, p. 202.
5 Rashi on *Bereshit* 4:22.
6 *Shemot* 20:22.
7 *Shabbat* 88a.
8 *Zohar* I, 125a.
9 Cf. Volume I, p. 259.
10 See Volume II, p. 80.
11 *Makkot* 11a.
12 Although David was not allowed to build the Temple, he could — and did — make all the necessary preparations for the building. See *Divre Ha-yamim* II, chap. 28.
13 *Sukka* 49a.
14 *Sukka* 53b.
15 *Tehillim* 120-134.
16 See *Be'ur Ha-gra, Orah Hayyim* 428 (end), *Siddur Ha-Gra, Ya'aleh Ve-yavo.* For interpretation see *Michtav Me-Eliyahu* III, p. 110.
17 *Bereshit Rabba* 13:13.
18 *Yalkut Shimoni, Noah*, no. 56.

19 *Bereshit* 7:12.
20 *Avot* 4:9.
21 *Hilchot Teshuva* 9:1. See Volume I, p. 38.
22 *Vayikra* 26:3-5.
23 *Kohelet* 7:14.
24 See "'Shop Window' for Evil," Volume I, pp. 74 et seq.
25 *Sukka* 12a.
26 *Bereshit* 7:11.
27 *Tanhuma, Noah*, no. 7.
28 *Mishle* 12:10.
29 *Aggadat Bereshit*, no. 4.
30 *Avot* 6:4.

□□□□□□□□□□□□□□□□□□□□□□□□□□□□□□□□□

The motives which led the people of Israel to make the Golden Calf have been the subject of much debate among our classical commentators.

In Volume II, in the article "Nature as Concealment of Miracle," Rabbi Dessler described four possible ways of looking at nature, corresponding, as he says, to four ascending levels of spiritual perception. In the article presented here, he uses these insights with great brilliance to elucidate the comments of Ibn Ezra and Ramban on the subject of the Calf — comments which had previously proved virtually incomprehensible to generations of students.

In the final paragraphs, Rabbi Dessler reveals what he means in practical terms by "living one's life on a supernatural level."

The golden calf

In his introduction to the *Laws Relating to Idolatry*, Rambam describes three historical stages in the development of idolatry.[1] (1) First, people had the mistaken idea that it was God's will that they should honor His ambassadors, the stars and the spheres (that is, the forces of nature), for the King is honored when we honor His ministers. (This is mistaken, because it is God's will that we approach Him directly.) (2) The second step was when, at the urging of false prophets and idolatrous priests, people began to worship the ambassadors (that is, nature itself), thinking that God had given them the power to bestow or withhold favors. (3) The final step was when the name of God was completely forgotten and the only gods recognized were the heavenly bodies (the forces of nature) and the idols which were introduced to represent them.

It is clear that the first error (stage 1) led inevitably to the worst excesses of idolatry (stage 3). We are now in a better position to understand what the classical commentators say about the sin of the Golden Calf.

In his lengthy comment on the episode of the Golden Calf,[2] Ibn Ezra makes the following important observations:

> God forbid, God forbid that Aharon should make an idol, or that Israel would want an idol. But they thought that Mosheh was dead…When they said …"[Make us] *elohim* who shall go before us," their intention [by the word *elohim*] was "glory residing in a bodily form" (*this means, to know the glory of God through reflecting on a form symbolizing the powers of nature — the ambassadors of Hashem; this will be more fully explained later*)…Thus it was made for the glory of Hashem; this was why Aharon built an altar before it and proclaimed that they would sacrifice on the morrow to the glory of Hashem…But owing to the influence of the mixed multitude…a small number of Israelites thought it was an idol…and said, "These are your gods, O Israel!"…The total number of those who worshiped the Calf as an idol was no more than three thousand[3] — one-half of one percent of the camp.

And earlier, in his comment on the final verses of *Parashat Yitro*[4] Ibn Ezra writes:

> "You shall not make [anything that is] with Me…" You saw that I spoke to you without an intermediary…you shall make no image…no forms to receive power from above, thinking that you are doing this for My glory, to be in a sense intermediaries between Me and you (*that is, in order to recognize Hashem by concentrating one's mind on them*), like the Calf which Israel made; for Aharon made it for the glory of Hashem…This is why He warns them here already not to make *elohim* of gold.

It is well known that at Mt. Sinai the people of Israel were on an extremely high spiritual level, the level meriting revelation of the Shechina; and their affairs were conducted by God on the level of open miracle. But when they realized that they were no longer sure of Mosheh's return, they thought they could no longer maintain that high level. Without the Divine aid that was channeled to them through the presence of Mosheh, they felt they were in danger of falling into the hands of the *yetzer*, and as soon as they had succumbed once, there was no limit to the depths to which they could fall. They therefore decided to descend to a more natural level of existence, where they would learn the presence of God from nature itself.

One whose true *madrega* is on the natural level can legitimately find spiritual fulfillment in recognizing God within the realm of nature. In the next generation we find, for example, in the episode of the "fiery serpents,"[5] that Hashem expressly commands the manufacture of a replica of a snake to be put on a pole,[6] "so that Israel might direct their attention heavenwards and subjugate their hearts to their Father in Heaven,"[7] that is, to impress upon themselves that afflictions of venomous snakes also come at the behest of Hashem. This is certainly very far from idolatry. According to the *halacha* there is nothing wrong in making the form of a snake, or a calf, provided it is not for the purpose of worship. The only images it is forbidden to make under any circumstances are the human form, and all four ḥayyot of the Heavenly Chariot (*Yeḥezkel* 1:10) — i.e., man, lion, ox, eagle — *together*.[8]

DESCENT INTO NATURE

But since *they* — the generation of the Exodus — were on a supernatural level, any descent into the realm of nature — even for an ostensibly worthy purpose — was counted *for them* as idolatry. This was their mistake. When Hashem "took us out of the rule of the stars and the host of heaven, which He apportioned to all the peoples under the heavens,"[9] the meaning is that He wished us to maintain ourselves on a supernatural level, while leaving the world of nature to the nations of the world, whose task was to see the work of Hashem in the midst of nature. (We certainly should not think that the meaning is that God apportioned stars, etc. to the nations for them to worship, since idolatry is prohibited under the Noachide legislation.) This is why idolatry is called *'avoda zara* — "strange service," not *'avodat sheker* — "false service"; there is a type of *'avodah zara* which is forbidden only to Israel, because it is "strange" to them according to their *madrega*.

THE DANGER OF DESCENT

But when one has descended to the level of nature, it is easy to become involved in the equivalent of idolatry, pure and simple, and to think that nature is the activating force. This, in fact, was the sin of the "mixed multitude," who said, "These are your gods, O Israel...." To live under the rule of nature is a great test. It is the test that was given to Adam: "By the sweat of your brow you shall eat bread." In his arrogance, man easily "goes into partnership" with nature and attributes all his achievements to his own efforts.

This is also the meaning of the words, "*These* are your gods, O Israel" — on which the Rabbis comment: "They desired many gods."[10] The Rabbis equate arrogance with idolatry,[11] and we have seen above how scientific and technological advances can feed human arrogance to a dangerous extent.[12]

One who stands this test *can* rise to the level where he sees the power of Hashem working *within nature*. But someone whose proper level is the supernatural is not permitted to descend to this test. This would resemble the first stage of idolatry which we referred to before, when people thought that they were honoring God by showing reverence for His ambassadors; but it was a brief step from that to real idolatry.

A SUBTLE DIFFERENCE

Following along these lines, one can trace a subtle difference between Ibn Ezra and Ramban in their modes of interpretation of the sin of the Golden Calf. When explaining his idea of "glory residing in a physical form," which we quoted earlier, Ibn Ezra adds: "And if you will reflect on the first journey, you will understand this." By "the first journey," Ibn Ezra refers to the journey of the Israelites from Sukkot to Etam, at the edge of the desert, when "Hashem was going before them by a pillar of cloud by day, to lead them on the way; and by a pillar of fire by night, to give them light."[13] In his comment on that verse Ibn Ezra writes: "Hashem was going before them…for the power of Hashem was going with the people of Israel; in the manner of the verse, 'He brings forth His glorious arm at Mosheh's right hand.'"[14] The meaning is that they saw the power of God in the very fact that Mosheh was leading them. Here, too, they say, "...*Elohim* that *shall go before* us," meaning that they wish to see the glory of God in those very natural phenomena which would accompany them.

RAMBAN'S VIEW

But Ramban writes: "However [Ibn Ezra's] explanation does not seem right to me. The Calf was not made in pursuance of the science of planetary influences [astrology], so that glory should reside in its form ...but their purpose in making that form was to concentrate on its meaning by means of its service; and I have already explained the secret of the first journey."[15] And on the meaning of that "first journey" Ramban writes:[13] "It is quite true that it is in the manner of the verse, 'He brings forth His glorious arm at Mosheh's right hand'; but not as he [Ibn Ezra] understands it. The verse also writes: 'So You led Your people to make Yourself *shem tiferet* (a name of glory).'"[16]

The difference between their interpretations lies in a very subtle point.

HIGHER AND STILL HIGHER

The highest level of recognition of God is when a person engages in natural physical activities, recognizing the whole time that all he achieves comes from God above. But here, too, there are two possibilities. We have written elsewhere[17] about the man at the keyhole who sees a pen writing, and who has only to open the door to see the person holding the pen. He illustrates one who sees only natural forces operating. When the door of truth is opened, he sees that in reality it is God who acts, holding nature like a pen in His hand. But there is a still higher level; that is, the one who sees that it is not accurate to compare natural causes to a "pen" in the hand of a writer. The pen is, after all, a necessary implement without which the writer cannot perform his task; while God does not require natural causes, neither does He make use of them. His will suffices to carry out all that He wishes. The fact that we see natural causes operating simply means that there is something wrong with our eyesight.

REALITY OR UNREALITY

The Torah obliges each one of us to carry on our lives by reference to natural causes. Adam's lot — "by the sweat of your brow shall you eat bread" — applies to us all. The difference between the two levels just mentioned is this. The person at the lower level, since he believes in the efficacy of natural causes, will find this mitzva perfectly understandable. On the other hand, the person on a higher level, who realizes the essential unreality of natural causes, finds this mitzva difficult to understand — a ḥok like the mitzva of the Red Heifer. He knows that Hashem does everything without needing to resort to "causes." His will is the direct cause of all things [except, of course, those things which He has deliberately left to human free will: "All is in the hands of Heaven except for the fear of Heaven"]. He is aware that there is no logical reason why the effect should follow the cause; the whole system of apparent cause and effect is erected by Hashem to form a background for our moral choices and the exercise of our free will.

This explains the argument of Ramban against Ibn Ezra in *Parashat Beshallaḥ*.[13] From the comment of Ibn Ezra it might appear that he is referring to the lower of the two levels mentioned above. He mentions the verse "He brings forth His glorious arm at Moshe's right hand,"[14] from which one might understand that they saw Mosheh as an instrument — a cause — interposed between Hashem and themselves. To this, Ramban cannot agree. The meaning is "not as Ibn Ezra understands it" (i.e., the verse), but only insofar as it is consistent with the other verse, "So *You* led your people...,"[16] that is, without any suggestion of an intermediary.

BASIS OF THE DISPUTE

And this very difference is reflected in their respective conceptions of the sin of the Golden Calf. Ibn Ezra understands that the wish was to involve themselves in a more natural life style, while at the same time learning that God alone does everything, nature being no more than an instrument in His hands. To this Ramban objects: "The Calf was not made in pursuance of the *science* of planetary influences [i.e. astrology]...but to concentrate on its meaning by means of its service." In other words, they made it as a means of attaining the highest level at which a person acts in the world, knowing all the time that there is no reality in his actions. Ramban makes one more very subtle point. He mentions that the form of a calf was chosen to accord with the ox — one of the four *ḥayyot* (living beings) which bear the Divine Chariot.[18] It is well known that this form stands for God's conduct of the world by natural means.

THE POWER OF THE DESTROYER

Ramban's comment contains a most difficult and obscure passage. He writes:

> Aharon's motive was this. Since Israel was situated in a wild and desolate desert... he thought that the destroyer would show the way in the place of destruction, for that is where his power is great; and when they would serve God there, He would pour upon him a sublime spirit such as was imparted to Mosheh.

On the face of it, it seems difficult to find any meaning in this passage. But we have to know that it is not enough to recognize that natural causes are unreal. We must be able to perceive that those natural causes which seem so constructive in the world, are in reality destructive.

It must be so, because all that is constructive and beneficial in the world comes from the goodwill of Hashem. Anything that in any sense lessens the revelation of God's glory cannot obtain goodwill from Hashem and hence must be destructive. Strictly speaking, therefore, a person who adopts natural means to maintain his life — for example, he ingests food in order to live — is apparently acting in a way which ought to diminish his life; for life comes directly from Hashem and not through the medium of food. If, by following the natural course, he is going to lose sight of this basic truth and become convinced that life depends on natural causes, he is endangering his life. Of course, it *looks* as if life depends on natural causes; it is an observed fact that if one does not eat, he dies. But we must realize that this sequence of events is decreed by Hashem, as a test for us. It is clear from the Torah that this is not an absolute law but only a test, for the Torah tells us that when a person reaches a certain very high spiritual level — a level which is described when Mosheh went up the mountain to be with God — he can abstain from food for long periods without dying, so long as he remains on that level. And at that level he does not even need manna, for even manna, which is spiritual food, is still in some sense a test.

It follows that the ingestion of food should bring about a person's death, for it possesses the power of destruction. It is poison to the soul. Why then does a person not die when he eats? Because Hashem has decreed this as a law, inscrutable as a *ḥok*.

NOT BY BREAD ALONE...

There is a verse in *Parashat 'Ekev*[19] which deals with this very subject, but which is frequently misunderstood. The verse reads:

> He made you hungry and he afflicted you and then He gave you the manna to eat...so that you might know that *man does not live by bread alone, but man lives by all that proceeds from the mouth of God.*

People usually interpret this verse to mean that of course a man lives on bread, but he cannot live *solely* on bread; he needs spiritual food, too. "All that proceeds from the mouth of God" refers to the mitzvot of the Torah, and these are the spiritual food that a man needs for his mental and physical health.

But this is a mistaken interpretation. When the verse says "Not by bread alone, but by all that proceeds from the mouth of God," it implies that bread, too, is something that "proceeds from the mouth of God," that is, that eating is a mitzva. It is only by virtue of God's command that we have to eat, and it is *this command* that gives us life, not the bread. But not only *this* command gives us life, says Mosheh Rabbenu, but "all that proceeds from the mouth of God," all the other mitzvot, too, give life to man. (It is true we see materialistic people, who have no conception of eating as a mitzva, and animals who also live when they eat; but this is part of the challenge of this world, which was created on physical lines to provide opportunities for free will.)

AHARON'S MOTIVES

Now perhaps we can attempt to understand the remarks of Ramban on Aharon's motives. The desert, which is a place of desolation where the power of destruction is manifest, is a good place to learn the vanity of natural causes. Aharon thought that if Israel would withstand their test there, and there come to recognize that the powers of nature have no reality, they would then reach the highest level and perceive that nature is actually destructive, and Hashem alone creates and sustains everything. Through this they might become worthy of having the spirit of God poured out upon them as it had been imparted to Mosheh.

(Ramban continues: "I have already explained the

secret of the first journey. [*This has been discussed earlier*] God forbid that Aharon would wish to compare himself to him [*i.e., to Mosheh*] but he wished to take something from him [*i.e., to emulate Mosheh in some sense*] so that their travels should derive from that attribute [*i.e. the attribute of* shem tiferet *mentioned in Yesha'ya 63:14, denoting the direct experience of the glory of God*]." The meaning is that even at that high level, at which nature is completely negated, there are still two possible ways of looking at the matter: one is called "the clear window glass" and the other "the unclear."[20] During their first journey while departing from Egypt, when Mosheh was in charge, they experienced the revelation of the Shechina with complete clarity. However no one could approach Mosheh's level, and Aharon merely hoped that they might attain a sense of God's guiding presence that resembled that first experience, even though with less clarity.)

THE FIRST STEP

It follows that both Ibn Ezra and Ramban agree that Israel's chief sin in making the Calf lay in their deliberately exchanging their previous high level for a more "natural" level. Even though they meant well, thinking that in this way they would be better able to maintain their service of Hashem in the absence (as they thought) of Mosheh, this still counted as a grievous sin, akin to the first step towards idolatry as described by Rambam in the passage cited at the beginning of this article. [These were the people's intentions; it was they who insisted on the calf symbol, not Aharon. (See

Ramban on *Shemot* 32:22.) Aharon had ideas of a much more elevated kind, as we saw earlier.]

What we have just described is a tactic frequently adopted by the *yetzer ha-ra'*, which tells a person to "play it safe" and run his life on "simpler" lines, rather than take the risks involved in a life devoted solely to Torah. For example, it may suggest to a person that if he adopts a life of *Torah v'derech eretz* (i.e., a more bourgeois lifestyle with, by natural standards, a more soundly based livelihood), he will make a greater *kiddush Hashem* [because he will show that one can be a successful businessman or professional and *still* be a fully observant Jew. This will raise the prestige of Torah observance].

We have explained elsewhere[20] that Adam's first sin was similarly motivated — a "going down" in level in order to "go up" to a much greater *kiddush Hashem*. Repentance for this kind of sin is very difficult, since it contains an element of "sinning with the idea of repenting."[21] There is no doubt that its origin lies in the cunning of the *yetzer*, whose avowed aim is to cast a person down from his high level and reduce him to a level of rank materialism.

Sincere reflection will reveal the true designs of the *yetzer*. One will discover that hand in hand with the imagined high motivation goes the simple desire for more material self-indulgence. Hava revealed this when she saw that "the tree was good to eat and desirable to the eyes" (it gratified the will for material pleasure), "and that it was wonderful for gaining understanding" (it provided the illusory motivation of rising to much higher intellectual attainments).[22]

And so it is with everybody. When one descends to the imaginary *Torah v'derech eretz*, there, under the guise of supposedly high ideals, lurk the lusts of this world.   □

notes

1 *Hilchot 'Avoda Zara* 1:1-2.
2 *Shemot* 32:1.
3 Ibid. v. 28.
4 *Shemot* 20:20.
5 *Bamidbar* 21:6.
6 Ibid. v. 8.
7 *Mishnah, Rosh Hashana* 3:8.
8 *'Avoda Zara* 43b; *Shulḥan Aruch, Yoreh De'ah* 141:4.
9 See *Devarim* 4:19-20.
10 *'Avoda Zara* 53b.
11 *Sota* 4b.
12 See Volume II, pp. 254, 266.
13 *Shemot* 13:20-21.
14 *Yesha'ya* 63:12.
15 On *Shemot* 32:1.
16 *Yesha'ya* 63:14.
17 Volume II, pp. 247-8.
18 *Shemot Rabba*, based on *Yeḥezkel* 1:10.
19 *Devarim* 8:3.
20 *Yevamot* 49b; see *Michtav Me-Eliyahu* II, pp. 208, 211.
21 See *Yoma* 85b, (Mishna).
22 *Bereshit* 3:6.

Free Will

The problems involved in establishing the freedom of our will, a principle of prime importance for *mussar* and all morality, were always in the forefront of Rabbi Dessler's concern. The origins of this discourse, like the origins of the "Discourse on Lovingkindness,"[1] go back to his Kelm years. This part, with its companion, "The Nature of Free Will,"[2] developed and reached their final form in England in the early years of World War II.[3]

The solution proposed here (in chapter 2) to the philosophic problem of determinism *versus* free will bears a striking resemblance, in its basic approach, to that proposed by Immanuel Kant. The notion of the ego which inhabits an "inner world" beyond the reach of the senses is strongly reminiscent of Kant's transcendental ego, which is above and beyond the world of phenomena, and yet is a necessary condition for all experience. Here, too, as in Kant, we find that causality is relegated to the sphere of sensual perceptions, while the ego, being beyond all sensory experience, maintains its freedom.[4]

Shall we asssume that Rabbi Dessler arrived independently at a similar solution to Kant's? Or was he familiar with Kant's writings? This writer does not think he was. But we have it on good

Discourse on free will

PART II: FREE WILL AND CAUSALITY

□□□□□□□□□□□□□□□□□□□□□□□□□□□□□□□□□

authority[5] that Rabbi Dessler's brother-in-law, Rabbi Doniel Movshovitz, who headed the Kelm academy between the wars, was well-versed in Kant's writings, to the extent that he could, and on occasion did (in private discussions with students), quote sections of them by heart. It seems possible, therefore, that Rabbi Dessler may have heard of Kant's solution from this source.

In his synthesis of the two perspectives in chapter 3, Rabbi Dessler, of course, goes far beyond Kant. Towards the end of this volume[6] we shall see how Rabbi Dessler was able, later on, to present this same solution in kabbalistic terms.

1   □□

the self-deception involved in raising the problem of causality versus *free will*

We have explained at length in "The Roots of Mussar"[1] that before one has gained control of one's *middot* and subjected them to the pure striving for truth, his opinions cannot possibly be true. He sees only what he wants to see and arrives at those conclusions which he desires. He is bribed by his *middot* and is partial to his desires. "Bribery blinds the eyes of the wise"[2] is an immutable law.

This is why we sometimes find clever people delving into difficult philosophic problems and coming up with acute and sophisticated results, while the critical observer can detect that the solutions have been arrived at on the basis of unconscious bias. *Middot* have been at work, subtly influencing the reasoning process. Sometimes people may hold contradictory opinions at different times, as it suits their purpose and bias. One may be completely convinced that his conclusions are based on pure logic while actually they stem from pure self-deception.

There is no area of thought where this is more evident than in the case of "free will *versus* determinism." There were and still are great philosophers who, because of this problem, have denied the reality of free will and human responsibility. They assert that man is but a plaything in the hands of natural causes, and any idea he may have of claiming credit for his actions is purely illusory. But at the same time the same person will, in the most egoistic manner possible, take pride in his intellectual achievements and claim credit for his professional success. And here the critic must raise his eyebrows. How can the thinker have forgotten so soon that he has just demonstrated, to his own and other people's satisfaction, that man is nothing but a machine, a stimulus-response mechanism? Can a machine claim credit for its predetermined activities? This only goes to show how people dominated by their *middot* cannot be trusted. Their unconscious bias determines their opinions; truth takes second place. This is hardly what we mean by objective thinking and the sincere search for truth.

This attitude is quite widespread and is by no means confined to philosophers. If a person does something for which others applaud him, he will have no hesitation in taking all the glory for himself. But if he commits a crime and is found out, his ego suddenly takes a back seat. If all else fails, he will try to avoid responsibility by hiding behind a deterministic shield. That is how philosophic problems can be used to promote a permissive life style. And of course, with characteristic inconsistency, the same person will claim credit for his "discovery," which he knows will be applauded by all like-minded people.

But this tactic is not new. Already some eight centuries ago Rabbi Baḥya wrote in his classic *Duties of the Heart*:[3]

> [The *yetzer ha-ra ʿ*] will cast you into the sea of doubts concerning the problem of determinism and personal responsibility. When he sees that you are inclined to deviate from the path of true service...he will try to convince you with cogent arguments that all human action is predetermined...so as to lessen your personal responsibility...If he notices that you are pursuing some mundane, material goal, he will encourage you to pursue it by all means, saying: Don't slacken your efforts; it all depends on you; ...you can achieve it if you want to. Success or failure is in your hands; exert yourself to the full; you will certainly attain all you desire of the pleasures of the world. So [the *yetzer*] reverses his arguments at will; sometimes adopting a deterministic approach, and at other times an approach based on the effectiveness of human action; with the

sole object of confusing you and drawing you along the path *he* wishes you to follow.

2   □□□

analyzing the problem

If we look at the problem objectively, we shall see that both ways of looking at things — the "free will" approach and the "causal" approach — have a certain validity in our lives.

When we look into our own minds, we observe firstly "selfhood" — our own ego. This ego presents itself as "I — my sense of being," "I — a recipient of the messages of sense perception," "I — who exercise free choice."

We are aware of all these aspects of the ego immediately, that is, without the mediation of the senses within ourselves and deriving from ourselves alone — that is, what we call "inner perception."

We also have senses through which the ego becomes aware of its surroundings, and intellect, with which the ego can think and reason.

Our senses can perceive only the externals of objects, never their true essence. This we call "outward perception." Every concept, judgment, or conclusion that the intellect constructs on the basis of sense perception can, thus, only be one based on "outward perception." All the concepts of science are of this kind.

"Inner perception" — awareness of self — is not mediated by any of the senses nor by all of them together. It is internal, intuitive knowledge, located in our essential selves.

Outward perception does not exist for the self except in association with inner perception, such as when we say "I see." But even so, *that which is seen* is perceived only externally; it is outside us. Our ego is not perceptible to external observations at all. That which is the basis of all observation cannot itself be observed, just as a camera cannot photograph its own photographic process. It can photograph only that which is outside itself.

CAUSALITY

"Cause and effect" is something we are aware of by external observation. We see that all changes in the physical world are connected in ways which we interpret as causal. We tend to generalize from this and to assume that physical causality is universal.

But our awareness of free choice comes to us by way of inner perception; we experience within ourselves the power and the freedom to act or to desist, as we wish.

It has already been explained that "inner perception" cannot be grasped by "outer perception." These two modes of perception are distinct aspects of the human mind. To the superficial view they seem to contradict each other, but in reality there is no contradiction. They are two independent faculties, each of them valid in the appropriate context. If one person reports the length of a brick as four and one-half inches and another as three inches, we do not assume a conflict of evidence. We realize that they must have been viewing it from different angles. It is the same with the inner and outer modes of perception. The attempt to refute one mode by reference to the other is as absurd as the argument of the blind philosopher who insisted that the sense of vision was unreal because he could not experience it by the sense of touch.

The ego makes use of the intellect to clarify the details and effects of the things brought to its notice by the senses. The ego also uses the intellect for matters connected with the objects of one's inner experience, such as free will, reponsibility, remorse, hope, avoidance of error, and so on.

So the intellect serves both modes of perception, but it does not grasp the essence of either of them. It cannot conceptualize the experience of selfhood with its concomitant free will etc. Neither can it conceptualize the act of sense perception. The intellect can analyze only those concepts which it constructs. A triangle, for instance, is a mental construct, and the intellect can define and analyze it. A pure sense-datum, like a red visual field, however, cannot be analyzed by the intellect, nor can it be defined in terms of simpler components. Perceptions such as these are the building blocks out of which the intellect constructs its world.

How then is it possible to argue that the experience of free will is an illusion because it cannot be conceptualized? Sight and touch, in essence, cannot be grasped by the intellect. The intellect must assume them in order to be able to think about the world.

If anyone maintains that our experience of free will is false because it is contradictory to the causal concepts of physics, he might just as well maintain that our experience of "the present" is also contradicted by physics. In geometry, a line has length but no breadth, and a point neither length nor breadth, but only location. In the same way you can divide time into past and future, and the present will then be nothing but an imaginary line — before a person could experience it, it would already be in the past. Should we then say that the present is an illusion? Then we don't exist in time at all. But the essence of our experience of time and all the riches of our existence lie just in those precious moments of "the present." If we did not exist in the here and now, past and future would have no meaning either. Rather, we must say that the experience of "present" may not be explicable in physical terms which apply to the external world, but that this does not matter.

This experience is real relative to ourselves: this is how we are, this is how we live our lives. It is true for our inner selves, and the laws of physics have no relevance in this context. So it is with free will, the truth of which we experience inwardly with reference to ourselves, and it does not matter if it cannot be comprehended by the concepts of physics.

There are some who go so far in their arguments against free will that they deny the very existence of the ego. But it is hardly worthwhile to argue against such absurdity. It is surely clear that if our experience of "ego" is false, then the experience of "I am," "I see", "I act" are also false. "Being" ceases to exist, and the "causes" and "effects" of the physical world also have no validity, since there is no one to experience them …and the problem, too, no longer exists.

3   □□□

the two modes united in their purpose

A house may be constructed of several thousand bricks, but the house is much more than the bricks. Here again we have two modes of perception. One can perceive the individual bricks, in which case one does not see the house. Or one can see the house, in which case one is not conscious of the individual bricks.

Sometimes when looking at something as a collection of individual objects, one may find that the component parts seem to be in conflict with one another. On looking at it as a whole, however, one finds that the conflict is resolved. A clockwork mechanism, for example, consists essentially of a mainspring which provides the motive power, and a series of gear wheels and ratchets which slow down the motion. Someone who is ignorant of the purpose of this mechanism will be puzzled. "If they wanted the spring to turn the wheels, why did they arrange things to slow the movement so drastically?" Only a person who is aware of the purpose of the clock will understand the need for these apparently conflicting factors.

The case is similar in the matter under discussion. Someone who has no idea of the unifying purpose which these two different modes of perception serve, will see a conflict. He may come to the conclusion that one of the two is false and illusory. But this would be extremely shortsighted. The two modes of perception — the outer and the inner — are both needed. They are unified by the purpose which they serve.

Both are needed to enable a human being to reach his final goal. Ego-consciousness and awareness of free will are needed for a sense of obligation and responsibility. The perception of causality (not as an absolute, but within the bounds we have described) is also necessary so that we may discern the hand of God behind the causes. We may thereby also come to recognize the First Cause, Who created and maintains in existence and supervises everything. By contemplating the vast and intricate causal network of creation, we bow our heads in gratitude before Hashem and realize our own limitations, as the Psalmist said: "When I see Your heavens, the work of Your fingers, the moon and stars that You have established — what is man that You should take note of him?..."[4]

The inner service of man depends on a proper balance between these two modes — on the one hand, to realize the power and responsibility of one's ego, and on the other, to negate all feelings of self-importance. One has to know that *all* comes from Hashem, and yet be fully aware of one's awesome responsibility. This is what we see when we look at man as a whole. Awareness of ego and awareness of causality are two faculties implanted in a person. By making use of both, each in its proper context, one reaches one's goal in this world.

Of course, it is possible to do the precise opposite, and make use of each in the manner prescribed by one's *yetzer ha-ra'*. When dealing with causality one can see only the causes and effects, without seeing the First Cause; that is, one can adopt a merely "natural" viewpoint. He will then view his ego as the source of power by which he can subdue nature, ignoring obligation and responsibility. Unfortunately, this is the viewpoint of too many people, leading them to irrational behavior, God-denial and materialism. ☐

notes (to foreword)

1 Volume I, part 1, p. 119; Volume II, part 2, p. 131.
2 Volume II, p. 49.
3 See Volume II, p. 48.
4 See Immanuel Kant: *Kritik der praktischen Vernunft* (1788), sec. 167-8.
5 Personal communication by Rabbi Dr. E. Blumenthal, who was a student at Kelm during 1936-39.
6 See p. 224 et seq.

notes

1 Volume I, pp. 161 et seq.
2 *Shemot* 23:8.
3 Section on "Integrity of Action," ch. 5.
4 *Tehillim* 8:4. [The perception of causality is essential also as a basis for moral responsibility. If there were no causal framework, the consequences of all actions would be unpredictable and no one could be held responsible for the "consequences" of his actions. Freedom of will makes sense only in a causal universe. — A.C.]

Recompense

The first essay in this series, "Being and Having," is, I think, unique in the whole of our literature, in that it attempts to give a reasoned, logical account of the development of the consciousness of a *tsaddik* in the World to Come. It is also a tremendous work of the imagination. Its breathtaking sweep and daring vistas challenge our humdrum ideas, and are powerful enough to revolutionize our thinking. These ideas, in embryonic form, were first developed and discussed among the circle of *talmidim* in Chesham, England, in 5700-5701 (1940-41). They were recorded (in the very brief form then customary) in a special notebook marked "Deeper Matters," whose contents were not for general circulation.

In its present form, it was first presented at the Gateshead Kolel during the winter of 5708 (1948) on three successive *Shabbatot* (*Parashot Va-yeḥi*, *Shemot* and *Va'era*). It was then written out in full by Rabbi Dessler personally, one copy being sent to his circle of *talmidim* in Ponevezh Yeshiva, Bnei Brak. This was the text, word for word, that was published in *Michtav Me-Eliyahu* Volume I, pp. 284-95.

In the present rendering it has been found necessary to abbreviate some parts of the essay. In

Being and having

□□□□□□□□□□□□□□□□□□□□□□□□□□□□□□□□□□□□□□□

particular, the description of the cyclical process in *'Olam ha-ba* has been somewhat simplified on the basis of some later writings of Rabbi Dessler on this subject.

The Hebrew title is *Havaya Ve-hassaga*. Now *"havaya"* is certainly "being," but *"hassaga"* is perhaps more accurately rendered by "obtaining," "grasping," or "acquiring." However "Being and Having" was thought more appropriate.

1 □□□

life in the World to Come

What is this thing which we call "life"? All that we know as "life" can be summarized in the following categories:[1]

(1) The intuition of our existence: ego-consciousness. This is the awareness of "being."
(2) Awareness of the ego's relations with the world outside itself in three modes:
  (a) Awareness of what we lack, both in the physical

and the spiritual sense, that is, awareness of need in relation to our being;

(b) Awareness of an urge to fulfill our need;

(c) Awareness of the actual fulfillment of the need.

These three belong to the realm of "having."

These perceptions of "being and having," or "the ego and its progress," are life itself (not just some aspects of life). What a person yearns for *is* his life. If his yearning is for vanities of this world, his life itself is vanity; if for spiritual things (the World to Come), his life partakes of the nature of the spiritual world.

ETERNAL LIFE

We say in the blessing over the Torah, "…Who has implanted within us eternal life." This means the yearning to make progress in the matters of the spirit. Things are planted in order to grow. What is the nature of the growth of this eternal life that has been planted within us? This will be explained, God willing, in the course of this essay.

All mundane acquisitions remain outside us; they can never become part of our being. Even the honor which we receive, perhaps the most abstract of worldly acquisitions (though we enjoy it no less for that reason), resides in others and not in ourselves.

KNOWING AND BEING

On the other hand, all spiritual acquisitions reside in ourselves, in our very being. By "spiritual acquisitions" we do not mean spiritual concepts which we grasp with our *intellect*. These do not become a part of *ourselves*.

[What we know intellectually has no power to influence our actions; it is as if the part of us which *knows* is not the same part which *acts*. Thus knowledge is not part of our real selves.] Neither do we mean mere emotionalism and enthusiasm. These are not "acquisitions" either, because they are transient; they tend to cool off very quickly. What we mean by "spiritual acquisitions" are those spiritual attainments that have become internalized to such an extent that one could not imagine oneself without them. An act is done *lishmah* when it is done as a matter of course, when the good deed is not seen by the doer as deserving special credit; just as one does not feel proud at being able to see or hear — on the contrary, inability to see or hear is perceived as a defect. The level of *lishmah* and the level of attainment called "the World to Come" are known to be identical;[2] they represent selfhood, "being."

RETURNING KNOWLEDGE TO ONE'S HEART

It follows that physical concerns are subject only to "having"; we desire them and obtain them, but they can never attach themselves to our being.[3] Spiritual matters, on the other hand, may be subject either to "being" or "having." We may grasp them first with our intellect, we may be emotionally aroused to aspire to them, but they still remain outside us; and this is what is called "having." Afterwards we may succeed in "returning them to our hearts,"[4] until they become real within us and part of our being, as we have explained before. These two concepts are clearly distinguished in the well-known verse [which concludes the first paragraph of the *'Alenu* prayer]:

You shall know today
And return it to your heart
That Hashem is the Almighty God
In heaven above and earth below;
There is no other.[5]

"You shall know today" refers to intellectual knowing;
"you shall *return it to your heart*" means making it a
reality in your inner self.

In a similar vein we find in the first Psalm:

But in the Torah of God is his delight
And in his Torah he meditates day and night.[6]

Our Rabbis take "his Torah" to mean "the student's
Torah" and comment that at first we are conscious of
studying "the Torah of God" — it is still something
alien to us. Later on we assimilate it and make it a part
of ourselves — it is "our Torah" that we are learning.[7]

MAKING ONESELF

Something great and wondrous can be learned from
this. *It is within a person's competence to make himself*,
to extend and enlarge his very being. He can "return to
his heart" all the knowledge gained by Torah study,
which then becomes an addition to his own very being.
(It is inaccurate to think that Torah knowledge is
"acquired" by receiving it into our minds as information, like the intellectual attainments of worldly matters. True, grasping Torah intellectually, externally, is
of this nature; but acquiring Torah in our heart is a
spiritual acquisition, of the nature of the World to

Come; that is, it becomes part of our self and our essence.)

The performance of mitzvot, too, has the power to convert a person's theoretical knowledge of Torah into permanent reality in his heart. By this pathway, too, Torah knowledge can be changed into real being.

This is the meaning of Rabbi Ḥayyim of Volozhyn's famous remark that when the Rabbis said "the reward of a mitzva is a mitzva" they meant the reward is the mitzva itself.[8] When a person performs a mitzva *lishmah* he *is* already in the World to Come without knowing it. Later, when he leaves the body, it will become clear to him. A great man once said that it is not that the *tsaddik* is in the World to Come but the World to Come is in the *tsaddik*. That spiritual essence that is within us is the stuff of the World to Come — the attachment to truth, the attachment to Hashem.

"HAVING" IN THE WORLD TO COME

In view of all that has been said, it may be surprising that we *do* find the idea of "having" in connection with the World to Come. The Rabbis said, "Better one hour of repentance and good deeds in this world than all the life of the World to Come."[9] The reason given is that mitzvot done *lishmah* are a form of attachment to Hashem, i.e., "being," while the World to Come is "having." Similarly, the *tsaddikim* in the World to Come are pictured as "sitting and enjoying the splendor of the Shechina"[10] and this is explained in our sources as a kind of mental process, an experience of delight which is a form of "having." (This must be so, because in "being," which is clear and obvious to a person, there can be no enjoyment. Pleasure and enjoyment are experienced only when something is obtained after it has been lacking.)

THE RHYTHM OF LIFE

However, this is the explanation. Just as life in this world consists of a constant interaction between "being" and "having," so does life in the World to Come. In this world spiritual progress consists in first absorbing knowledge intellectually, and then "returning it to one's heart" so that it becomes part of one's being; then absorbing intellectually still higher knowledge, and returning this, too, into his heart, and so on, in an unending process. Similarly in the World to Come, the *tsaddik* does not remain stationary. He is involved in a continuing upward progression. (There is an allusion to this in the Divine promise addressed to Yehoshua' the High Priest: "I will give you *mahlechim* (walking, movement, progress) among these who are *'omedim* (standing, stationary)";[11] meaning that even when you enter the world of truth and find yourself in the company of angels, who remain stationary and experience no change or progress, *you* will be able to go forward and pursue your upward path. And again, "Those wise in Torah have no rest in this world nor in the World to Come, as it says, 'they shall go from strength to strength...'"[12])

Let us reflect on this somewhat more deeply and maybe we shall succeed (with God's help) in understanding it a little better.

SPLENDOR OF THE SHECHINA

Upon entering the state known as "the World to Come" the *tsaddik*, as we saw above, begins to "enjoy the splendor of the Shechina." God raises, so to speak, a corner of the curtain, and the *tsaddik* experiences a little of God's greatness, of His overwhelming, many-faceted love for His creatures. He gets an inkling of the majestic universal plan which God has for all His creatures, and derives unimaginable joy from the realization that his struggle with his *yetzer ha-ra'* in his previous state has significantly contributed to the fulfillment of that plan. His soul is suffused with unutterable delight.

And another thing, the very fact that he is granted such revelations, the very fact that he is privileged to experience so much pleasure must mean (he realizes) that his past efforts are appreciated. To know that Hashem, whom He served, is pleased with him adds immeasurably to his satisfaction.

GRATITUDE

If this is all there was, 'Olam ha-ba would be a somewhat static situation. However, the *tsaddik* does not rest there. Having cultivated, in his previous state, the very fundamental virtue of gratitude,[13] he begins to realize that the reward he is being given is vastly in excess of what he deserves, and he is overwhelmed with thankfulness. Realizing his own worthlessness, he becomes all the more aware of God's unbounded love poured out so abundantly on someone as unworthy as he. The intensity of his gratitude grows, until it leads to a state of self-abandonment before Hashem. This is the way of Yisrael: "When they are given greatness, they make themselves small before Hashem."[14]

PULSATING RHYTHM

The more gratitude a person feels for past favors — the more he abandons "himself" — the more he can be given. Consequently Hashem now reveals more of His glory to the *tsaddik*, whose soul is again delighted by an intensified experience of the splendor of the Shechina. This leads to further gratitude and self-abnegation, and this in turn to further delight, and so on, in the pulsating rhythm which is the *life* of the World to Come.

Now the experience of enjoyment is "having" (we speak of "having enjoyment"), while gratitude and the abandonment of self are "being." Like life in this world, so, too, life in the spiritual world consists of a continuing interplay between "being" and "having," in an ever-ascending spiral. This is the potential for unimpeded and eternal growth implanted in us by the Torah and mitzvot which Hashem has given us.

TIME IN *'OLAM HA-BA*?

On the verse "The days of David drew near to die,"[15] our Rabbis say:

> Do days die?…When *tsaddikim* die their days are annulled but *they* continue to exist; as it says, "They exult on their couches, with the praises of God in their throats." We learn from this that even when dead they praise Hashem.[16]

"Their days are annulled" means that they no longer exist in a time-frame as in this world, but the process of spiritual growth that we have described, in which "having" alternates with "being," implies some form of time reference. We shall discuss this further in part 2.

'OLAM HA-BA IN THE TSADDIK

It must be understood that the states of "being" attained in 'Olam ha-ba are a direct reflection and consequence of the states of "being" attained in this world by Torah and mitzvot learned and performed lishmah. As we have seen, the dynamic process of 'Olam ha-ba is powered by the states of being, and these states of being are in fact identical with the states of lishmah attained by the tsaddik in this world. In this sense we can understand the saying, "Rather than the tsaddik being in 'Olam ha-ba, 'Olam ha-ba is in the tsaddik." In this world, however, the full implications of these states are concealed from the tsaddik. They and the experiences they induce are fully revealed to him only in the World to Come. All the wondrous processes of life in the World to Come are seen therefore, at every stage, to be direct developments of the mitzvot one acquired during his life in this world. In a sense it is his 'Olam ha-ba that he experiences. Thus, the shame of completely unearned benefit is avoided.

Who can describe, who can imagine, the immensity of joy the tsaddik experiences in that world, the unutterable happiness of everlasting spiritual progress! Who can possibly describe the development of his being from stage to ineffable stage, punctuated by ever-renewed, sublime spiritual experiences! To know

it one has to live it. It is not accessible to the outside
eye. "No eye but Yours, O God, has seen it."[17]

Each item of a person's Torah and mitzvot, each
point of self-conquest in his upward progress in this
world, forms a separate root out of which eternal progress will grow in the World to Come. Each occasion on
which he conquers his *yetzer* for the sake of God forms
a new facet in the revelation of God's glory, from which
an upward spiral of the spirit will ensue in the future
world — and not from each separately, but from all of
them together, their combination creating a qualita-
tively different and unimaginably more intense field of
light.[18] If we manage to fill our lives here with such
points of light, what a tremendous life of spiritual
progress can we expect in *'Olam ha-ba*!

2   □□

a deeper insight

Pleasure arises from a desire fulfilled. The greater the
obstacles in the way of fulfillment, the more intense the
pleasure when those obstacles are finally overcome.

Similarly in the life of the spirit, each victory in the
battle of the *yetzer ha-ra'* gives pleasure. When a person
is faced with a great temptation and summons up all the
forces at his disposal, including motivations of reward
and punishment, and succeeds in gaining his victory,
the ensuing pleasure is all the greater. A person on this

level can also take pride and pleasure in the mitzvot he
has accumulated, just as on a lower level people take
pride in accumulating material wealth.

BEING AND *DEVEKUT*

But a person who has arrived at the level of *lishmah* no
longer experiences any resistance to doing mitzvot. It
is simple and obvious to him that the will of Hashem
must be done, and he does it. His urge to do mitzvot
comes from no selfish motive; it is for the love of
Hashem, pure and simple. He lives on the level of
"being," not "having." Feeling no resistance to the
doing of the mitzva, he also feels no pleasure in the
completed acts. As we know, it is only "having" which
engenders pleasure, not "being." In "having" there is
novelty; in "being" there is no novelty. What was first
thought a great achievement is now taken for granted.
The novelty is gone.

In the state of "being" one tends to lose one's sense
of self. This self-abandonment is equivalent to a state
of attachment to Hashem (*devekut*). It is egotism that
separates us from Hashem and the more we reduce our
egotism, the closer we are to Hashem. This state of
attachment is a state of "being," and therefore does not
give pleasure. Pleasure has no part in it.

When we consider these lofty levels of "being" we
ask ourselves: If this state of sublime attachment to the
Divine has no enjoyment in it, what is the point of it?
This question betrays our selfish pettiness. It shows
how far we are from the world of selfless love which
expects nothing in return. *We* are worried by the ques-

tion: So what do we get out of it? — we, the pleasure seekers...distant from the Divine...so far from *being*.

Every human being is born into a given environment, and is given specific physical and mental powers and tendencies, all of which determine his level of *beḥira*.[19] He is free to use them either to rise from this level or to fall from it. In theory a person could fall so low that he would lose all contact with spiritual life. However, as we have previously discussed,[20] the people of Israel have been promised that they will never be permitted to fall that low. "Even when they are in the land of their enemies [*in the sense: even when they are in the power of evil influences*], I have never rejected them...to utterly destroy them...."[21] Evil has no power to remove the last vestige of holiness from the heart of Yisrael. We often see, in fact, that Jews who have apparently lost all contact with Torah life still retain a natural affinity for charitable deeds and humanitarian activities of all kinds.[22]

We find in our sources that there exists a point of truth in every Jewish heart that is never extinguished, and can never be reached by the *yetzer ha-ra'*. This is the point of inwardness — of "being" — which is the inalienable property of the Jewish soul and which accompanies us in the World to Come.

The same sources tell us that even those who, according to the Mishna, have "forfeited their share in the World to Come,"[23] have forfeited only the share that should have been theirs by virtue of their service in

this world, but they still have a share from "the trea-
sure house of free gifts."[24] The "free gift" is that holy
point of inwardness which is there from birth. It is a
point of "being," but since it was not developed by
them during their lifetime in this world, it lacks the
capability of growth in the World to Come.

MINIMUM GROWTH-POINT

However low a person stands on the ladder of *beḥira*, if
he has made only the slightest attempt to raise his level
by freely chosen acts during his lifetime, if he has
achieved even a minimal point of "being" by his own
efforts, this point will have the capability of growth
and will ensure him — within the bounds of that particular point — an everlasting life-process in *'Olam ha-ba*.

We are told that in the time of Rabbi Yose there were
gangs of robbers who lived in the mountainous areas of
Eretz Yisrael and waylaid unsuspecting travelers, took
their possessions and then murdered them. Some
members of the gangs were Jews, who plundered and
murdered like their companions. However, if the way-
farer turned out to be Jewish they refused to ill-treat
him in any way, but insisted on leading him back to the
road until he was out of danger. Rabbi Yose remarked
that, for this, these robbers were worthy of entering
the World to Come.[25]

This seems to us most extraordinary. But in the light
of the above, if these robbers overcame their evil inclination on *their* level of *beḥira*, and succeeded in converting their love for their fellow Jews into a point of
"being" within them, we can understand that their

portion in the World to Come can contain the seeds of infinite progress.

Here we can see the enormous difference between an "earned" and "unearned" 'Olam ha-ba. The latter remains static, while the former leads to an infinite expansion of consciousness into an unimaginably glorious future. Effort is the secret. We must never be complacent, never rely on the good qualities we already possess. Only by constant effort at improvement in this world will we ensure a life of spiritual growth in the World to Come.

NEW PERSPECTIVE

We promised to discuss in this section the problem of time in 'Olam ha-ba. This is part of a larger problem. Adam and Ḥava lived (apparently) a physical existence in Gan 'Eden. We learn from our sources that had death not been decreed on them because of their sin, they would have entered 'Olam ha-ba on that very Shabbat. How is it possible to enter 'Olam ha-ba with a body?

If we analyze this problem carefully we may arrive at a completely new perspective on the concepts "physical" and "mental." We use the term "physical" to describe anything that can be perceived by the senses. We reserve the terms "non-physical" or "mental" for thoughts, feelings, ideas and aspirations, since these are not sensible objects, even though the content of the ideas or aspirations may be very physical or materialistic. From a higher viewpoint, such as that of Adam before the sin, this is not so.

If a person were to see an angel in the guise of a human being (like the angels who appeared to Avraham) we may be sure that the bodily guise would be bodily in all respects — it would have weight, one could touch it, etc. Yet it would be hard to say that it is really physical, since we know that it is merely a disguise which will disappear the moment there is no need for it.

"AS IF"

From the higher standpoint this is precisely how one views our "oh so solid" physical body. It is a mere appearance, an "as if," which is maintained so long as it serves its purpose. Our Rabbis have said: "There is no artist like our God. A human artist can paint a picture on a wall but he cannot make it [come alive]…Our God makes a picture within a picture and makes it [come alive]…"[26] A great man once commented on this: A great artist can paint a picture so life-like that at a distance one can be deceived into thinking it is real, but when one gets closer one soon sees one's mistake. When God makes a picture it is so life-like that one can go right up to it, feel it, perceive it with all one's senses — it looks and feels absolutely real. But in reality, it is only an "as if." Our body is that picture.

From that perspective, what is termed "physical"? Physical thoughts, material desires, selfish motives — these "bodily" aspects of the mind are what is called "the body." And what is death? In the common view it is the corruption of the body. But on a higher level this is not death at all; this is merely changing a garment. Death occurs when selfish bodily characteristics remain in the mind, for this is the corruption of the mind. The *tsaddik* who completely conquers all his selfish desires does not die: "Yaakov Avinu did not die."[27] "*Tsaddikim* even in their death are called alive."[28]

TIME-SENSE AND INTELLECT

Therefore, if Adam had not sinned, he would have reached perfection and immediately cast off his illusory garment and entered *'Olam ha-ba* with all his mental faculties unimpaired. The "body" he would have taken with him would have been those "lower" mental faculties: the sense of time, and the intellect. (We call these "lower" because they are more connected with "having" than with "being.") And these are indeed the faculties which every *tsaddik* takes with him to *'Olam ha-ba* and which make possible the tremendous growth-progress we discussed in part 1.

The *rasha'*, on the other hand, who misused his intellect in this world, will find that his intellect is unavailable to him in the World to Come, as we discussed in a previous section.[29]

It follows that the more we avoid selfish material aspirations and the more we follow our spiritual ambitions, the closer we approach the level of *Gan 'Eden* and the further we get from death. The Gemara describes the comparative ease with which *tsaddikim* leave this world when their time comes to depart.[30] This is because the aspect of [spiritual] "death" in their lives is minimal. The four who died only because of "the counsel of the serpent"[31] had reduced this "death" aspect to the absolute minimum.

3

being and having in this world: rest and joy

"If one comes across a problem in Torah learning which has no solution, then you can be sure the problem itself is the solution."[32] The meaning of this paradox is as follows. There are three ways of raising and solving difficulties:

(1) Some criticize in a negative way, implying that the source must be wrong. This is *apikorsut*.

(2) Some consider the difficulty to the best of their ability until they eventually come up with a solution.

(3) If the difficulty is so strong that no solution is apparent even after deep reflection, some will turn the difficulty against themselves. They will attribute failure to their own lack of merit, in the manner of the great *gaon* Rabbi Akiva Eger,[33] who concludes his most devastating *kushiyot* with the words "I have not the merit to understand this; may Hashem enlighten my eyes." In this sense it is said that the problem itself is the solution, for it proves that one has not yet succeeded in considering and understanding the matter properly.

WHEN THE PROBLEM IS THE SOLUTION

Similarly it is so in the realm of historical events and the Divine conduct of the world.

(1) The *apikoros* sees only the dark side of life; he

does not want the light, for the *yetzer ha-ra'* within him shuns the light.

(2) One who sees the ebb and flow of God's self-withdrawal and self-revelation (the "problem" and the "solution") and constantly strives for better understanding will eventually be granted this understanding. This will cause him great joy, for "there is no greater joy than resolution of doubts."

(3) The one who looks from the higher vantage point sees that the difficulty itself is the solution. This is the man who has no high opinion of himself and therefore directs his criticism only against himself. He is the person who has reached inwardness, *lishmah*, attachment to the Divine. In this sense the problem is the solution. By criticizing himself he reveals his own "nothingness," and this, as we have seen, is the essence of attachment to Hashem.

God's essence cannot be grasped by our intellect, but *devekut*, inward attachment, is directed to God Himself. (When the Rabbis said that "You shall attach yourself to Him"[34] implies "attach yourselves to His ways of lovingkindness,"[35] they meant that we should emulate His ways from a deep love of Him Himself — because they are *His* ways.)

SHABBAT AND YOM TOV

This is the main difference between *Shabbat* and *Yom Tov*.

The essence of *Yom Tov* is joy — "You shall rejoice in your festival."[36] This is joy in achievement, in "having." Thought, vivid imagination, clear conception — these all give great joy.

On the other hand, the essence of *Shabbat* is rest, *devekut*, "being." This is self-abandonment, which is higher than achievement.

On *Shabbat* it is "as if all your work is done,"[37] nothing is lacking; what lack can there be when one is "attached" to one's God? All is done, all is over; one needs nothing when one is alone with one's Creator. Selfish aims, ambitions, work, are all without value. This is akin to Rabbi Shimshon Rafael Hirsch's concept of the prohibition of *melacha* on *Shabbat*. The Torah wants us to refrain on that day from all productive human activity, he says, in order to demonstrate God's mastery over the world. Some kabbalists have also written in this vein.[38] It is also in this sense that we are to understand the *Shabbat* resembles *'Olam haba*.[39] □

notes

1 Compare p. 177.
2 See Rambam, *Commentary on the Mishna*, end of *Makkot*. See also *Strive for Truth* Volume II, p.36.
3 See Maharal, *Be'er Ha-gola* (London 5729), p.32.
4 See also p. 19.
5 *Devarim* 4:39.
6 *Tehillim* 1:2.
7 *Kiddushin* 32b, and Rashi ad loc.
8 *Ruah Hayyim* on *Avot*, beginning.
9 *Avot* 4:17.
10 *Berachot* 17a.
11 *Zechariah* 3:7.
12 *Berachot* 64a.
13 See Volume I, p.147.
14 *Hullin* 89a, based on *Devarim* 7:7 — "for you are the smallest of all nations."
15 1 *Melachim* 2:1.

16 *Yalkut* ibid., based on *Tehillim* 149:6.

17 *Yesha'ya* 64:3.

18 See the last article in this volume.

19 See Volume II, pp.52-56 for a full discussion.

20 See "The Blockage of the Heart," p. 63. See also Volume I, p. 180.

21 *Vayikra* 26:44.

22 See Volume II, p.132.

23 *Sanhedrin* 10:1.

24 *Midrash Talpiot, ḥelek* no.8.

25 *Zohar, Midrash Ha-ne'elam, Bereshit* 118a.

26 *Megilla* 14a.

27 *Ta'anit* 5a.

28 *Berachot* 18a.

29 See p. 27.

30 *Berachot* 8a.

31 *Shabbat* 55b. (The four were: Binyamin, Amram, Yishai and Kil'av son of David.)

32 R. Nahum Z. Sieff, in the name of his father, R. Simḥa Z. Sieff.

33 He lived 1761-1837.

34 *Devarim* 13:5.

35 Rashi ad loc.

36 *Devarim* 16:14.

37 *Mechilta, Yitro* 20:9.

38 See R. Mordechai Alter of Ger, *Sefat Emet, Yitro*, 5665 etc.

39 *Mechilta, Ki Tissa* 31:13.

□□□□□□□□□□□□□□□□□□□□□□□□□□□□□□□□□□□

I recall asking Rabbi Dessler, not so long after I
had begun studying under him in London in the
early 1930s, whether his *mussar* was of the hellfire
variety. "What is wrong with hellfire *mussar*?" he
replied. "If you are aware of the consequences, you
don't do many sins."

In fact, neither the deliberate, didactic *mussar*
of Kelm, whence Rabbi Dessler came, nor his own
highly sophisticated *mussar* philosophy, bore the
slightest resemblance to that other variety, if
indeed such a variety ever existed. Nevertheless,
the problem of sin and its consequences was never
far from his mind.

In the time of Rabbi Yisrael Salanter, when
every observant Jew believed without question
that sinners were punished in Gehinnom, the
problem facing Rabbi Yisrael was how to bring
that belief to bear on the actual behavior of the
believers. In Rabbi Dessler's time, the problem
was somewhat different. People were not sure how

Gehinnom —
concept and application

□□□□□□□□□□□□□□□□□□□□□□□□□□□□□□□□

to understand the tradition, especially since there
are differing and apparently conflicting statements in various sources.

In the previous article, "Being and Having,"
Rabbi Dessler made a daring attempt to give us
some insight into the mind of a *tsaddik* in *'Olam
ha-ba*. In the present article, composed in Bnei
Brak in 5709, he tries to do the same for the mind
of a *rasha'*. The article has been curtailed in accordance with the requirements of the present
volume.

□□□

We mentioned in a previous article[1] that the variety of
explanations and similes given in our sources for the
concept of Gehinnom stems from our inability to grasp
purely spiritual states. We have to try to understand

them by analogy. We can appreciate, for example, that the burning remorse that may fill our consciousness *then* is many times worse than the experience of physical pain *now*. Let us attempt to explain some of these apparently conflicting descriptions.

FIRE

The Gemara says: "Fire is one-sixtieth of Gehinnom."[2] [This means that the experience of being burnt by fire gives us a mere inkling of the intensity of mental pain in the World to Come.]

My saintly great-grandfather, Rabbi Yisrael Salanter, and my father-in-law's father, Rabbi Simḥa Zissel, of blessed memory, revealed to us the tremendous importance of the imagination as a tool for progress in spiritual life. We are an amalgam of the "mental" and the "physical," and our physical aspect is affected more by sensory impressions than by ideas. We remember them, of course, but we prefer the visual impression to the mental one. We have no inclination to forget our loved ones, but still the memory fades and a picture keeps it alive.

In spiritual matters we have never seen the object of our thoughts, and there are many powerful forces inducing us to forget it. These forces have all the vividness of sensory experience on their side. What chance is there for a mere idea, a mere thought, to hold its own against these?

To deal with this very serious and basic problem, these masters of *mussar* advocate the use of the imagination, which can be an extremely potent mental force.

They tell us to make as vivid a mental picture as possible of the idea we wish to "return to our heart."[3] This image-forming process should be undertaken without haste and in as much detail as possible. There is then a good chance that it will be grasped by the "physical" side of our being [corresponding to the subconscious mind]. This is the essential innovation of the *mussar* movement initiated by Rabbi Yisrael Salanter.

It will be readily understood that the comparison between Gehinnom and physical fire lends itself very readily to an imaginative exercise of this sort. Rabbi Yisrael recommended that the mental picture be itemized as much as possible and the process should consist of a large number of small steps. Thus: first, one should imagine how much it would hurt to hold one's finger in fire for one second; then, for two seconds; then for three...and so on. This exercise should be pursued without haste, with a pause after each step to allow the effect to sink in, until one eventually reaches twelve months.[4] But fire is only one-sixtieth of Gehinnom. One can rethink the whole exercise for a fire twice the intensity of ordinary fire, then three times, then four times, and so on.[5] If one succeeds in building up a complete imaginative picture of this sort, one can be sure that it will be extremely effective.

Rabbi Yisrael added that one should also consider that time seems longer to someone in pain. If one is lying awake with a toothache during the night, how long it seems until morning! One thinks hours have passed and looks at his watch to find it is only a few minutes. In one's imagination, the twelve months of Gehinnom should expand accordingly.

SIN

Rabbi Avraham Azulai writes:

> The *yetzer ha-ra'* is itself Gehinnom....[It] has many powers.... They seduce, they punish, they are Gehinnom; it is all one.... Defilement itself destroys its bearer.[6]

In a similar vein Rabbi Ḥayyim of Volozhyn writes with reference to the *mishna*, "The reward of sin is sin,"[7] that the true punishment of a sin is the sin itself.[8]

As the *Midrash Rabba* puts it, in more picturesque terms:[9]

> The *tsaddikim* are pictured in their abode: "In a goodly pasture I will pasture them and in the high mountains of Israel shall be their dwelling."[10] And the *resha'im* are pictured in *their* abode... "On the day he goes down to She'ol...I covered him with *tehom* (the deep abyss)..."[11] Just as a jar is earthenware and is covered with earthenware, so the *resha'im*... "Their deeds are darkness; they say, 'Who sees us? Who knows of us?'"[12] Since they are dark, God brings them down to She'ol which is dark and covers them with *tehom* which is dark, as it says, "And darkness was on the face of *tehom*."[13]

Here again the message is the same; the sin and the punishment are one.

The Zohar, too, tells us that "Gehinnom is fired by the fierce heat of the *yetzer ha-ra'* of the wicked...by day and by night it is not subdued."[14] [The meaning is that since the only true existence is attachment to holiness, and only this gives true happiness and satisfaction for all eternity, sin and defilement can only detract from one's existence and destroy one's happiness, the pain being in proportion to the depth of the sin. What we call punishment is thus really only an effect.]

The purpose of Gehinnom is to "burn away" the part of one's personality corrupted by sin, as the surgeon cauterizes a wound which has festered. [This applies only to those sins for which one has not repented in this world. By the pain and remorse of *teshuva* one cauterizes the wound oneself.]

Most people do not live a life of unrelieved sin. When the evil has been burnt away, the Torah and mitzvot which they made part of themselves during their lifetime come into their own and they can enter their 'Olam ha-ba, as discussed in the previous section. Regarding those who have no such spiritual acquisitions to fall back on, the Gemara tells us that, after their twelve months in Gehinnom, "their body comes to an end, their soul is burnt, and they become ash under the feet of the *tsaddikim*."[15]

This hints at the idea that even so, not quite all is lost. They will still find some ultimate purpose. Their ash will form a path for the feet of the *tsaddikim*; that is, their very failure will serve as an object lesson from which the *tsaddikim* will learn the truth of God's justice.

But even apart from this, Gehinnom has an end for each person according to his individual state. For some this may be the inextinguishable point of truth in the Jewish soul which we discussed in the previous section.[16] Similarly we learn that Avraham Avinu saves sinners from Gehinnom if he sees they have not betrayed the covenant of circumcision.[17] Furthermore, if a *rasha'* has even a thought of *teshuva* during his lifetime, his Gehinnom will stop at this point.

We may learn from all this how much effort we should invest in reaching the inwardness of mitzvot: *Shabbat* which penetrates the heart, *teshuva* which enters the heart, perhaps a mere *thought* of *teshuva* — so long as the thought is an inward thought. Outwardness and insincerity will get us nowhere.

There is a "world of falsehood" and a "world of truth." People are under the impression that when they die they immediately enter the world of truth. This is a mistaken idea. To say that we are in the world of falsehood is the same as saying that falsehood is in us. We see the world with false eyes. The uncorrected evil in a person is the falsehood. Even in *that* world, so long as Gehinnom has not burnt away the evil, falsehood still rules within. One is still subject to contradictions, lies, insincerity and outright dishonesty.

To cite one example, the Gemara reports that Onkelos — when he was considering becoming a proselyte — established contact through necromancy with Titus and Bil'am. They both told him of the torments they were suffering for attacking Israel during their lifetimes, but at the same time they advised him to hurt the Jews, or in any event not to join them.[18]

This insight may help us understand an enigmatic passage in one of our sources.[19] We are told that when *Shabbat* comes, bringing relief to those in Gehinnom, they are taken to two mountains of snow. At the end of *Shabbat*, when they are taken back, they try to take some snow with them to cool themselves during the week. Hashem says, "Woe to you, *resha'im*, you steal even in Gehinnom!" The language is, of course, metaphorical. On *Shabbat* the consciousness of the *resha'im* is raised so that they are able to appreciate to some extent whatever attachment to *kedusha* they may have had during their lives. This temporarily "cools off" the intensity of their remorse. The essential characteristic of a *rasha'* is the ability to convince himself that "bad" is "good," and in particular that he is not so bad as he really is. This characteristic accompanies *resha'im* even in Gehinnom and they would like to convince themselves — and if possible even God Himself — that the "snow" of *Shabbat* can protect them during the week. That is, that their momentary rise in *madrega* on *Shabbat* represents their true selves.

Rabba bar Bar Hana, on his travels in the Sinai desert, heard Korah and his company repeating over and over again the words: "Mosheh and his Torah are true, and we are liars."[20] If they have arrived at this recognition, why are they still in Gehinnom? Because their words are external to themselves, they are not yet completely sincere.

Our trouble is that we mix good and bad. We know perfectly well in our heart of hearts what the truth is, but we think we can change reality. This is the essence of wrong *behira* — to put falsehood in the place of truth.

Do we really take all this to heart? Does the dulling effect of habit lessen the *hillul Hashem*, or does it perhaps add to it?

DAY

Several aspects of Gehinnom are reflected in the following *midrash:*[21]

The orb of the sun has a sheath...In time to come the Holy One blessed be He will divest it of its sheath and allow it to burn up the *resha'im*, as it says, "And the coming day will burn them up."[22] R. Yannai and R. Shim'on say:...[this is] Gehinnom... [*The burning sunlight means the revelation of God's abundant mercy, which causes the* resha'im *terrible remorse.*]

Other Rabbis say: There is Gehinnom [*apart from the remorse due to the great light. This may refer to the fourth aspect of Gehinnom which will be discussed soon.*]

R. Yehuda ben R. Ila'i says: Neither day nor Gehinnom, but fire which comes forth from the body of the *resha'im* themselves and burns them up, as it says, "Spiritual fire shall consume them..."[23] [*This refers to the aspect of Gehinnom which is the sin itself.*]

The Gemara says in *Nedarim*[17] that the unsheathed sun that will burn the *resha'im* will have the opposite effect on the *tsaddikim*, bringing them healing and spiritual growth. It is clear (as we have indicated) that this refers to the great revelation of God's glory, which for the *tsaddikim* is a source of life and growth, while for the *resha'im*, that very revelation of the abundance of the love they rebelled against will cause them the burning pangs of remorse.

As we have mentioned above, these are not meant to be exclusive statements, but each represents one facet of the truth.

Another aspect of this idea is mentioned by Rabbenu Yona:[24]

The soul of the *rasha'*...will be taken up on high for judgment, and also to see *how it exchanged the heights for the depths*, as one sends a stone high in the air, only to see it descend again by its nature to the earth below

…as it says… "And the soul of your enemies He shall sling as in a slingshot."[25]

The revelation given to the *rasha'* is only temporary. He will soon again descend to his normal level where darkness predominates. But the memory of what he lost remains.

NOTHINGNESS

We find a further aspect of Gehinnom in the writings of the Maharal of Prague. He often refers to the fate of the *rasha'* after death as *he'der* — nothingness.[26] We shall endeavor to explain this concept. A human being has a great longing for contact with people and things outside himself. Solitary confinement is a great punishment for a person. But even a person in solitary confinement still has *some* contact with the outside world. He can see things and hear things in his cell and outside it, and he can think about them.

What if even these small points of contact with the world outside himself are removed? In recent years some people have experimented with "total sensory deprivation," a state in which the organism is prevented from receiving any sense impressions from the outside world. It has been found that such states impose intolerable psychic strains, and if persisted in can induce madness.

The *rasha'* in this world was interested only in worldly matters. Even when he is forcibly removed from these things by death, his interest in them remains. However, in his present state he soon realizes that he no longer has any access to these things which dominate his interest so much, or to any physical thing whatsoever. This is all gone like a dream. What is left is only his ego, his being, but this — of his own choice — is empty of real content, that is, of spiritual content. He has to live with himself, deprived of all relation to anything real and substantial. This is deprivation with a vengeance! This is what Maharal means by the Gehinnom of nothingness. □

notes

1 "Mental Attachment to Torah (2)," p. 26.
2 *Berachot* 57a.
3 See the previous article.
4 The time allotted for *resha'im* in Gehinnom. See *Rosh Hashana* 17a.
5 Compare postscript to "No Reward in this World," Volume I, pp. 34-35.
6 *Hesed l'Avraham, Massechet Gehinnom.*
7 *Avot* 4:2.
8 *Ruah Hayyim*, beginning; *Nefesh Ha-hayyim* 1:12.
9 *Bamidbar Rabba* 1:1.
10 *Yehezkel* 34:13.
11 Ibid. 31:15.
12 *Yesha'ya* 29:15.
13 *Bereshit* 1:2.
14 *Teruma* 150b.
15 *Rosh Hashana* 17a, based on *Malachi* 3:21.
16 See above p. 196.
17 *Eruvin* 19a.
18 *Gittin* 56a.
19 Source mentioned in note 6 (chapter 3).
20 *Bava Batra* 74b.
21 *Bereshit Rabba* 6:6. See also *Nedarim* 8b.
22 *Malachi* 3:19.
23 *Yesha'ya* 33:11.
24 *Sha'arei Teshuva* 2:18.
25 *I Shemuel* 25:29.
26 E.g., *Gevurot Hashem*, ch. 34.

Thoughts of
the true world

□□

"If your wish is not to die, die before you die."[1] The
meaning of this epigram is that if you wish to live the
true life of the spirit, die to those false wills which
deflect you from that goal. Try to acquire in this world
something of the outlook you will inevitably have
when you pass over to another state.

When a person passes over to that state, our sources
tell us that he has to undergo three successive correc-
tive processes:

> (1) *The grave.* A person has to recognize that he is no
> longer in this world and will never return to the body
> and its desires.
> (2) *Gehinnom.* To burn away the defilement of sin, by
> remorse at having acted against the will of Hashem.
> (3) *Bathing in the "river of fire."* This is to remove the
> last vestiges of attachment to the life of selfish in-
> terests.

To avoid having to undergo this long-drawn-out process of dying, we should try to acquire here and now attitudes which will prepare us for eternal spiritual life. □

notes

1 See *Tamid* 32a.

Worlds

□□□□□□□□□□□□□□□□□□□□□□□□□□□□□□□□□□□

The lecture on which the first article in this series is based was given at Ponevezh Yeshiva in 5709 (1949). It has been curtailed for the requirements of this volume.

Maharal's principle of relativity, as enunciated here, which sees all reality as relative to the observer, was considered by Rabbi Dessler to be an extremely important and fundamental insight. It is interesting to note that it foreshadows developments in scientific thought in the twentieth century, in the realms of relativity and quantum theory.

The worlds of *'Asiya* and *Yetsira*

ABSOLUTE AND RELATIVE CONCEPTS

□□

1   □□

the meaning of "worlds"

The four worlds of *Kabbala* (in ascending order:
'Asiya, Yetsira, Beriya, Atsilut) are neither places nor
universes; they are states of consciousness. Why are
they called "worlds"? What is the meaning of "spiritual
worlds"?

We have mentioned earlier that our awareness of our
self, our ego, is direct and immediate. It depends
neither on the mediation of the senses nor on that of
the intellect.[1] We may call this "absolute" knowledge.

Besides knowledge of our identity and the freedom
of our will, this inner awareness also includes moral
categories, such as justice and injustice. These could
not have arisen merely by conditioning and environ-
mental stimuli. Primitive man, when struck by his
neighbor, did not cry out merely because he was in pain
or because his dignity was hurt. Apart from this he
cried out that it was *unjust*. He felt that the principle of

fairness and justice had been infringed. Where could so abstract an idea have come from if not from a sense of justice deeply embedded in himself? As the verse says, "God made man *straight*...,"[2] i.e., with an innate sense of justice.

On the other hand, the ego is also aware of promptings mediated by the senses, which lead it to desire certain things or certain experiences perceived as pleasant or pleasure-bringing. These feelings may also be perceived as absolute.

It is here that people differ. For some, only their sense-mediated feelings are absolute, while their moral awareness is seen as extremely relative. (When someone hurts them they complain of injustice, but when they consider hurting someone else the injustice is not perceived.) For others, the moral imperatives are seen as absolute, and other considerations dwindle into insignificance.

What one sees as absolute constitutes one's "world." The person who sees sense-experience as absolute lives in the world of *'Asiya*. One who sees moral and spiritual awareness as absolute lives in a higher world — the world of *Yetsira*. Adam in *Gan 'Eden* and Israel at Mount Sinai lived in that world. For them, reality was the life of the spirit.

So writes Rabbi Ḥayyim of Volozhyn, commenting on the verse "And all the people saw the thunderous sounds..."[3]

> They heard what was [normally] seen and saw what was [normally] heard; that is, all their physical powers were extinguished and their mode of perception was greatly refined, so that *the reality of physical, sensible things*, which they had previously perceived with their senses,

was no longer apparent to their sense of vision and they did not notice them. For example, if someone had wanted to explain to them about physical matters he would have had to give them a verbal report [to assure them] that there were indeed such things in existence. But spiritual matters, which previously they would have been able to understand only by verbal explanations, were now accessible to them by vision in their wondrous new mode of perception.[4]

Rabbi Ḥayyim's remark that "they would not have noticed" physical things refers to the fact that a person sees only that which interests him; what is of no interest to him he can pass by without its making any impression on him. He can truly say, "I didn't see it." Most people are unaware of the make of suit on a passer-by in the street, while a tailor will notice every detail. This passage bears out the point we have been making — that what one perceives as "absolute" changes according to one's spiritual level.

2 □□

the "worlds" and free will

If we reflect more deeply we shall see that all inner awareness comes from the world of *Yetsira*, while physical sense-perception derives from the world of *'Asiya*. It follows that however closely a person is attached to his selfish desires and materialistic perceptions, his awareness of his own self, at least, is no outward perception and must come from the world of *Yetsira*. Thus, every human being has at least one spark from that higher world — his ego-consciousness.

If he decides to progress on the path of spirituality, all his perceptions may eventually become refined and true, and he may then find himself in the world of *Yetsira*. Alternatively, he may choose to defile himself to such an extent that he eventually loses all sense of spiritual perception. In that case, his spark from the *Yetsira*-world, his ego-consciousness, may be considered as if "in exile" among the powers of evil.

FREEDOM AND CAUSALITY

We have already discussed at length the problem — which we do not think is a valid problem — of causality *versus* freedom, or physical determinism in supposed opposition to free will.[5] The problem, as stated, is that if everything in the world is governed by causal factors, if each event is invariably brought about by an antecedent cause, or antecedent causes, what room is there for free will? Surely every human act is, in physical terms, an event, and therefore must have been produced by antecedent physical causes?

First of all, this question ignores the concept of the *beḥira*-point.[6] What is the *beḥira*-point? The point at which we feel an internal battle between the forces of good and evil. Where there is no battle, there is no *beḥira*. It may be there is no battle because that point has already been conquered by the *yetzer ha-ra'* — we no longer perceive that act as a sin. Or it may be that it is now in the domain of the *yetzer tov* — we have risen above that temptation.

We can now be quite sure that the type of people

who ask this question have already pursued their lusts without restraint and have never experienced a true *beḥira*. There is no doubt in their case that their desires and passions are the causes of their actions, to the exclusion of all possibility of free will.

But the person who is sensitive to moral issues and fights a hard battle in his heart to conquer his selfish drives — he will have no doubt about the reality of *beḥira*. He knows it from his own very real experience. (We have discussed these matters at length elsewhere.)[6]

But apart from these considerations, the insights we have gained in connection with the differing "worlds" show us that the whole problem is completely unreal.

The ego (the spark from the world of *Yetsira*) certainly experiences *beḥira*. Even if a person is compelled to do something under duress, he still feels that the choice is in his hands. He can choose to refuse to comply at all costs, or to give in. "Ego" means "I decide, I choose, I am responsible." If I do something which turns out to be to my disadvantage, I am annoyed with myself; and in the same way I expect others to behave responsibly, too. There is thus no doubt whatsoever that in the inner perception of the ego, free will is a reality. But the perception of causality derives from the physical, sensual side of my nature — the outer, not the inner sense.

Awareness of the freely choosing "I" is the spark that comes from the world of *Yetsira*. The perception of physical causality is rooted in the world of *'Asiya*. From the perspective of *Yetsira*, physical causality has no reality. So where is the problem? We do not consider it a problem if dreams contradict reality; similarly there is no problem if *'Asiya* seems to contradict *Yetsira*.

3   □□

relativity and reality

It is important to understand that all reality is relative to the observer. What I perceive as real defines my world, and this, in turn, depends on my spiritual level.

It should be realized that when Avraham and Yitzhak saw a cloud hovering over the mountain which beckoned them to the *akeyda*[7] while the "servants" (who were Eliezer and Yishmael[8]) did not see this, the "seeing" and the "not seeing" indicated their relative *madregot*. It would be a mistake to think that the vision was a mere hallucination. What they saw was the *reality* — of their world.

Maharal of Prague expounds this very fundamental truth in *Tiferet Yisrael*[9] and many other places. He emphasizes that human language always refers to the reality that is present to the human mind.

The Torah says, "And Hashem descended upon Mount Sinai." This has caused great puzzlement to commentators throughout the ages. In what sense can it be said that Hashem, who is beyond all time and space,[10] descends upon a particular mountain? Maharal says simply that since that was how it appeared to the human observer, that is the proper way to describe it. And, he emphasizes, this does not mean that it only "looked" like that but "really" it was otherwise. It was "really" like that, for reality is relative to the observer. We know no other reality than reality relative to ourselves.

Maharal also refers to the episode in the Torah where

Adam gives names to all the animals and birds.[11] He cites the *midrash* in which the story continues thus:

> [God said to Adam:] And what is *your* name? Adam replied: Adam, for I was created from the earth [*adama*]. And what is My name? continued God. And Adam replied: Adonai, for You are the Lord of all. God said:...The name that Adam gave Me — that is My name.[12]

This *midrash* is making a very profound statement, says Maharal. It expresses in allegorical terms the very point made above. Even Hashem can be spoken of only in relation to the observer — the human being.

We have already explained at length how this very fundamental principle can be used to understand the concept of the "worlds" of *Kabbala*. It will be found equally useful when attempting to understand on a more profound level references to angelic beings, miracles, prophetic visions, *sefirot* and the like.[13] Our hope is that when the intellect succeeds in grasping these profound truths, the heart will also succeed in converting the knowledge into "inner truth," capable of purifying our actions and our motives. □

notes

1 See "Free Will and Causality," chapter 2.
2 *Kohelet* 7:29.
3 *Shemot* 20:15.
4 *Nefesh Ha-ḥayyim* 3:11 (first gloss).
5 See "Discourse on Free Will, Part 2."
6 See Volume I, p. 53 and Volume II, pp. 52 et seq.
7 See the first article in this volume.
8 *Vayikra Rabba* 20:2.

9 Chapter 33.
10 I *Melachim* 8:27.
11 *Bereshit* 2:19-20.
12 *Bereshit Rabba* 17:4.
13 Sources cited in this connection in the original article include: Maharal, *Gevurot Hashem*, second Preface (on miracles); *Tsi-yoni, Parashat Va-yehi* (on appearances of *tsaddikim* after their deaths); Rabbi M. H. Luzatto, *Klah Pithei Hochma* nos. 7-8 (on reality of *sefirot*, etc.).

□□□□□□□□□□□□□□□□□□□□□□□□□□□□□□□□□□□

This impressive discourse was delivered by Rabbi Dessler soon after the founding of Gateshead Kolel in 5701 (1941).

It was in fact the second part of the opening discourse at the Kolel, "Obstacles to Repentance" (Volume II, pp. 75-84).

Unity of creation and
unity of the human heart

□□□

Hashem planned and created the universe as a vast organism with all its multifarious parts workng perfectly in conjunction. This is the significance of the remark in the *mishna*: "The world was created by ten sayings,"[1] the symbolism of "ten" being the combination of many units into a single whole.[2]

The whole of creation serves a purpose: the revelation of God's glory to His creatures.[3] There can be no greater lovingkindness than this. [God's glory is revealed to a human mind each time someone looks in wonder at the stars; each time — faced by a moral choice — someone chooses the good in honor of God; each time the hand of God is seen in history and in the workings of providence in each individual life. Even when the person fails to meet the challenge, God's guiding hand may be revealed; even in punishment, God's justice and truth are manifest.] Taken all in all, the number of such revelations is extremely high. We call each individual experience of revelation a *gillui*.

EACH IS UNIQUE

Why are there so many people in the world? Because each individual has his or her own part in the great plan of creation. Our Rabbis said, "Just as their faces are all different so are their minds never the same."[4] The infinite variety of facial appearance among human beings is but a symbol of their infinite diversity of mental characteristics: their varied gifts, talents, abilities, propensities and character traits which make the spiritual and moral challenges facing each individual absolutely unique.[5] God created this vast number of unique human beings for this very purpose — to provide so many multifarious facets for the revelation of His glory — *gillui kevod Hashem*.

Each moment of time presents for each created being a new opportunity to contribute to the Divine revelation. No two moments have the same revelation-content. "He renews the works of creation each day, continually"[6] means that every moment of every day is a new world. The purpose of the moment just past is not the same as the purpose of the present moment.

Should a person waste a moment, that portion of revelation is lost to him. It can be restored only by *teshuva*, or alternatively by punishment, which substitutes a revelation of God's justice for a revelation brought about by the person's good *beḥira*.[7]

PERMUTATIONS AND COMBINATIONS

How awesome and wonderful are the vast number of revelations of God's glory! The multitude of created beings is so enormous... millions upon millions... and the number of moments from the beginning of creation until the end of the 6,000 allotted years...in worlds upon worlds...And all of them, all, are nothing but *gillui kevod Hashem* — vehicles for the revelation of God's glory.

But this is not all. We have not yet mentioned the combination of revelations and their interactions. For revelations, like all spiritual matters, do not proceed merely by arithmetical progression. They double and redouble in an amazing geometrical nonlinear progression by innumerable permutations and combinations of all kinds. Each new combination is multiplied by the preceding one (for all are present in the memory simultaneously), and this new combination is multiplied by the next, and so on in a never ending, unimaginably sublime series of incomparable experiences.

Maharal adds that this is also the meaning of the conclusion of the *mishna* in *Avot*:[1] "And why was it created by ten sayings?...In order to reward the righteous who build a world fashioned by ten sayings and to punish the wicked who destroy such a world." Each action must not be taken in isolation, but in the context of the vast and awesome *gillui* that emerges from the interactions, combinations and recombinations of all the revelations of all times, all worlds and all creations.

There are factories that are organized in such a way that, for example, quantities of raw timber are delivered at one end; these are then automatically processed into logs, boards and eventually matches. These are mechanically dipped into sulphur and arranged in boxes, which emerge at the other end of the factory in cartons ready for delivery to the wholesaler. There are obvious advantages in such an arrangement. There is one disadvantage, however: if the slightest thing goes wrong anywhere along the line, the whole factory comes to a standstill.

There is a certain similarity in the structure of the spiritual universe. If one person destroys the *gillui* potential present in one moment, he has damaged the whole "factory"; the whole spiritual universe suffers as a result. The situation can be restored in only two ways: either by the *gillui* resulting from his *teshuva*, or by the *gillui* resulting from his punishment.

Here is an awesome revelation of the damage that can be wrought by sin. The sinner, in his arrogance, reveals separateness instead of coherence; he thus injures the basic structure of the universe. The angels "give permission to each other" to praise Hashem; they "receive the yoke of the Kingdom of Heaven from one another."[8] This demonstrates their will to identify with one another, to unite their acts of revelation so as to abolish all separateness. In our lives this translates as love of one's fellow creatures — "you shall love your neighbor as yourself."[9] There can be no acceptance of the yoke of the Kingdom of Heaven without all God's servants being united. My father-in-law's father, the revered Rabbi Simḥa Zissel, pointed out that even Israel at the Red Sea, to whom God's glory was revealed to a degree unequalled by the prophets,[10] sang their song *"all of them together"*;[11] only when they were completely united could the revelation be manifest.

This will shed light, too, on the *midrash* about the creation of man, when God said, "Let *us* make man…"[12] to indicate that He "took counsel" with the angels, teaching us that "a greater person should consult with a lesser person."[13] To take counsel with some-one means to include him in your decision. He should not feel that you are separating yourself from him, for only by united effort can the full revelation of God be obtained.

A human being is a universe in miniature. He possesses a multitude of mental powers, and many and varied are the facets of God's glory that can be illuminated by him — by his acts, his free choice, his intellectual and spiritual perceptions. But intellectual perceptions are not enough. God chose not intellectual achievements, but the perceptions of the heart. "And you shall know today" — but this does not suffice; above all — "you shall return it into your heart." How does a person return his knowledge into his heart? Only by learning *mussar*.

All his abilities and his brilliant mind will not help him. Intellect may fly high but only the heart can influence actions. "Returning the knowledge into one's heart" [which is only another way of saying: letting the knowledge in the conscious mind penetrate the subconscious] is achieved by use of the imagination. Vivid imagery combined with reflection can make a lasting impression.

HOW TO TALK TO ONE'S HEART

Reflection is effective only if it is attuned to the true level of one's heart. Is one's heart close to selfish, material interests? Then speak to it with imagery taken from that sphere. [For example, one can say to one's heart: "If you jump out of bed with such alacrity for such a petty thing, how much more for something you

know is so much more important." Or, "You want
happiness, satisfaction, reliable friends? I will show you
how you can gain these through Torah." And so on.]
The heart needs the intellect to guide it, but the intellect needs the heart to ensure that all its knowledge
becomes truly part of one's inner being. The intellectual person sometimes thinks it is beneath his dignity
to occupy himself with imagery geared to the subconscious mind. Nothing could be further from the truth.
The greater needs the lesser just as the lesser needs the
greater.

Here again we see that the true revelation of God's
glory comes about only through united effort. □

notes

1 *Avot* 5:1.
2 Maharal, *Netivot 'Olam, Netiv Ha-Torah* 1.
3 *Avot* 6 (end).
4 *Bamidbar Rabba* 21:2.
5 See "Why the Righteous Suffer," Volume I, pp. 87-88.
6 *Shaharit*, first blessing before *Shema'*.
7 Explained in "Mental Attachment to Torah, Part 1," in this
volume, p. 23.
8 *Shaharit*, first blessing before *Shema'*.
9 *Vayikra* 19:18.
10 *Mechilta, Beshallah*, no. 2.
11 *Shaharit*, blessing after *Shema'*.
12 *Bereshit* 1:26.
13 *Bereshit Rabba* 8:8. See Volume II, p. 76.

□□□□□□□□□□□□□□□□□□□□□□□□□□□□□□□□□□□□

This was one of the last lectures we merited to hear from our beloved *rebbe*. It was delivered in Ponevezh Yeshiva shortly before his death, in the winter of 5714 (1953).

This, too, has been somewhat abbreviated to suit the requirements of the present volume.

To unify God in love

□□

In the first sentence of *Mesillat Yesharim* we are told (*inter alia*) that before we can hope to begin the true service of God we must be absolutely clear about "what our duty is in our world." Elsewhere we have devoted a whole article to analyzing and reflecting on the profound words of Rabbi M.Ḥ. Luzatto in this opening sentence of his great *mussar* classic.[1] Here we will consider what is meant by "duty."

Are we really aware that we have duties? What do we mean by "duty"? Is it something like the obligation felt by the head of a family to provide for his family? But he loves his family. What one does to please oneself is not pure duty. Pure duty is the obligation of a slave who works for his master without expecting to get anything in return.

Very few people in our times feel any sense of obligation towards the Almighty. They do as they like. Our Rabbis said: "'You shall not go astray after your heart' refers to denial of Hashem; 'nor after your eyes' refers to sinful imaginings."[2] A great secret is revealed here: the denial of God precedes the sins of lust. The desire for freedom from obligations — which is the will to deny God — comes before the wish to gratify physical desires. The will to throw off all sense of duty is the strongest of all motivations. One would like to say to God, "You have no claims on me." We do not say this openly, of course. But within our hearts that thought lies hidden. The proof is that we do not feel any obligation towards Hashem, or if we feel it, we prefer to ignore it.

ENJOYMENT OF TORAH

Success or failure in the spiritual realm depends on our feelings of pleasure or pain. If one gets pleasure out of doing bad and feels pain in doing good — his downfall is assured. If he enjoys the spiritual life and Torah learning gives him pleasure, and on the other hand, wasting time causes him pain — he is on the rise.

The trouble is, that you have to labor in Torah before you can enjoy it. But there is a very effective and not very difficult way of overcoming this. One has to make it clear to oneself that the period of difficulty will not last long. This is not a trick. He should explain to himself that it will really be so. If he puts true effort into his learning, then in a very short time, even in a matter of weeks, he will find himself sitting happily, enjoying his learning.

MEANS OF ESCAPE

We live in a generation which has thrown off the yoke of Torah. But Hashem has left us one means of escape from this baneful environment. We have only to throw ourselves into Torah study, and very soon we will see how deep learning can become a joy to us. We will come to love it unreservedly, with God's help.

In the last few generations, by the grace of Heaven, a new method of learning has been given to us: the method of deep conceptual analysis called *derech ha-havana*. Heaven has provided us with a method of Talmud study that yields satisfying results for less effort. In an age when everything is made easy and there is an abhorrence of hard work, both physical and mental — and it must be admitted with regret that Torah circles also have not escaped this universal trend — this innovative approach to Talmud which has swept through *yeshivot*, has proved to be, literally, a godsend.

Of course strictly speaking, fear should come before love; that is, service out of a pure sense of duty (fear) should precede the period when one can enjoy a sense of achievement (love). In previous times, many years of intensive study and very considerable knowledge were needed before one could attempt to solve Talmudic problems on one's own. Nowadays the situation is different. In our time, when no one wishes to bear a yoke, we have been given great men of genius who have shown us a shortcut to Talmudic understanding (*havana*). As a result, it has become possible to achieve love and enjoyment of Torah in a much shorter time. To a certain extent, we have been able to bypass the stage of a rigid sense of duty, acceptance of the yoke of Torah out of *yir'at shamayim* and recognition of the Giver of the Torah.

But surely this presents us with a grave problem. At the beginning of this article we emphasized that without a strong sense of duty there can be no service of Hashem. How can we reconcile this with what we said before?

In the article "The Unity Principle through the Ages,"[3] we explained that the mitzva of unifying God takes on a different form in different ages to counteract the *yetzer* of that age. We said that in our age the mitzva is to devote ourselves to Hashem and His Torah.

But we learn in our sources that there is a "higher unity" and a "lower unity."[4] The higher unity means to unify God in love, and the lower, to unify Him in fear.

In the higher unity, the sense of duty and the love of God are not in conflict. The perfect service we spoke about at the beginning of this article meant that the servant of God should have no thought of self and his heart therefore would be open to the love of God. Love is duty and duty is love. This is unity indeed.

On the lower level, however, it is difficult to envisage unity altogether. Fear normally means that one is worried about oneself. Preoccupation with self means separation from God. Where is the unity?

LOVE AND FEAR

However, a person can have *yir'at shamayim* only if he in some sense already loves holiness. If he did not possess some sense of attachment to holy things, he would have no *yir'at shamayim*. One who is interested only in the material things of this world is convinced that he can get all he wants by dint of his own efforts; he does not look to God's providence. And he may well find the facts confirming his attitudes. (We wrote many years ago that a *rasha'* may be granted affluence in this world to serve as a "shop window" for evil.)[5]

The *yer'ei shamayim*, on the other hand, wishes to avoid such an outcome at all costs. He is not averse to having the good things of this life, but only if he can obtain them without breaking his attachment to *kedusha*. He does his duty out of fear — fear of losing his material affluence — but his fear is based on love (the basic love of holiness which he possesses, as we have explained). He, too, unites God in love and fear. This is the "lower unity."

THE TORAH STUDENT

The student of Torah in our time develops along a very similar pattern. The very fact that he is interested in Torah at all betokens a basic love for holy things. The modern world offers so many other attractions that only those with a certain affinity for holiness will be drawn to Torah in the first place. This love leads him to accept the yoke of hard work at the beginning. There may be a period in which he will see nothing but effort, with very little enjoyment, very little sense of achievement. If he perseveres during this period — the period of "duty", "labor" and "bearing the yoke" — he will soon arrive at the stage of enjoyment, love and satisfaction.

We can learn from this that even the lowest degree of

"yoke acceptance" must be built on some foundation of "love." We express this in our prayers:

> You have brought us near to Your great Name (*Sela!*) in truth, *to give thanks to You* [the higher unity], and to *unify You* [in the lower unity, even in a situation where God hides His face] *in love.*

notes

1 See Volume I, pp. 227-33.
2 *Berachot* 12b.
3 Volume II, pp. 231-34.
4 Zohar, *Berachot* 12b, 18b, etc.
5 See Volume I, p. 74.

comprehensive glossary
(*for volumes 1-3*)

The following glossary provides a partial explanation of some of the Hebrew, Yiddish and Aramaic words and phrases used in volumes 1-3 of this book. The spelling and explanations reflect the specific way the word is used there.

AGGADA (AGGADOT): Talmudic passages dealing with ethical or other nonhalachic topics.

AKEYDA: Abraham's binding of Isaac on the altar.

AMORA (AMORAIM): the Sage(s) whose traditions and opinions comprise the Gemara.

APIKOROS: a heretic; a non-believer.

APIKORSUT: heresy.

AVINU: our Father.

'AVODAH ZARA(H): idolatry.

'AVODAT HASHEM: service of God.

AVOT: (1) the fathers or Patriarchs; (2) the MISHNA tractate of that name.

BA'AL TESHUVA (BA'ALEI TESHUVA): one who returns to the Torah.

BAMIDBAR: the Book of Numbers.

BAMIDBAR RABBA: MIDRASHIM (expositions) on BAMIDBAR.

BATLAN: a good-for-nothing.

BEHIRA: free will; free choice.

BEIT HA-MIDRASH: a place of Torah study.

BEN TORAH: one devoted to Torah.

BERESHIT: the Book of Genesis.

BERESHIT RABBA: MIDRASHIM (expositions) on BERESHIT.

BITTUL TORAH: the misuse of one's time in non-Torah pursuits.

CHAMETZ: leaven.

COHEN: see KOHEN.

DERASHA(H) (DERASHOT): (1) discourse; (2) derivation.
DERECH ERETZ: (1) courteous behavior; (2) earning a livelihood.
DEVARIM: the Book of Deuteronomy.
DEVEKUT: ecstatic devotion and attachment to God.

ELLUL: the month before TISHREI.
EMUNA: faith.
EYCHA: the Book of Lamentations, read on *Tisha B'Av*.

GALUT: Exile.
GAN EDEN: the Garden of Eden; Paradise.
GAON (GEONIM): (1) a genius in Torah learning;
   (2) Sage(s) of Babylonian yeshivot.
GEHINNOM: Hell.
GEMARA: Talmud.
GILLUI: revelation (of).

HA-: the.
HALACHA (HALACHOT): (1) the entire body of Torah laws and instructions; (2) a specific Torah law.
HAMETZ: see CHAMETZ.
HASHEM: God (colloquial).
HASSID (HASSIDIM): one who goes beyond the letter of the law in all matters.
HAS(S)IDUT: (1) the behavior of a HASID; (2) the Hasidic movement.
HAYYOT, HAYYOT HA-KODESH: "living beings" perceived as carrying the Chariot of God in the vision of Yehezkel (chap. 1, vv. 5-14).
HAZAL: an acronym meaning "Our Sages, of blessed memory."
HEIMISH: (Y.) lit., homelike; simple, warm, unpretentious; Eastern European.
HEREM: ban.
HESED: lovingkindness.
HILLUL HASHEM: desecration of the Divine Name.

HOK (HUKKIM): a statute of the Torah; a law not easily understood by the human intellect.

HOSHANA RABBA: the seventh day of SUKKOT.

ISSUR: prohibition; forbidden act.

KABBALA: works of Jewish mysticism.

KARET: excommunication of the soul.

KASHRUT: observance of the Jewish dietary laws.

KAVOD: honor; glory.

KEDUSHA(H): holiness.

KELI (KELIM): an instrument; an implement; a vessel.

KERIAT SHEMA': the recitation of the SHEMA'; or the portion of the Torah commencing with "SHEMA'" (*Devarim* 6:4-9).

KEVOD: the glory of.

KIDDUSH HASHEM: sanctification of the Divine Name.

KIYYOR: the laver (washbasin) in the Sanctuary.

KLAL YISRAEL: the community of the people of Israel.

KOHELET(H): the Book of Ecclesiastes.

KOHEN (KOHANIM): priest(s).

KOHEN GADOL: the high priest.

KOLEL: institute for advanced Talmudic learning.

KORBAN: sacrifice.

KUSHIYOT: difficulties; apparent contradictions in Jewish learning.

LASHON HA-RA': speaking [badly] of another person.

LATKE: (Y.) pancake.

LECH LECHA: "Go away [from your land]" (*Bereshit* 12:2).

LEHAVDIL: lit., to distinguish; an apologetic phrase used when mentioning holy and unholy matters in one breath.

LISHMAH: "for its own sake"; from unselfish motives.

LULAV: a palm branch used during SUKKOT.

LUZ: "indestructible" bone.

MA'AMAR: an essay.

MA'ARIV: the evening prayer service.

MA'ASER: a tithe.

MADREGA(H) (MADREGOT): spiritual or moral level.

MANNA: the sustenance given by God to the Jews in the desert.

MASHIAH: the Messiah.

MELACHA: work; especially that forbidden on SHABBAT.

MELACHIM: Kings.

MIDDA(H) (MIDDOT): character trait; disposition; attribute.

MIDRASH (MIDRASHIM): (1) an exposition of a scriptural verse; (2) a compilation of such expositions.

MIKVEH: an immersion pool for ritual purification.

MINHA: the afternoon prayer service.

MISHKAN: the Tabernacle.

MISHLEY: the Book of Proverbs.

MISHNA: the Oral Law edited by R. Yehuda Ha-Nasi.

MISHPATIM: civil statutes.

MITZVAH (MITZVOT): a commandment of the Torah.

MOSHEH: Moses.

MUSSAF (MUSSAFIM): additional offerings / prayers on Sabbaths and Festivals.

MUSSAR: (1) moral discipline; (2) the ethical movement founded by Rabbi Yisrael Salanter in the 19th century.

NEFESH: the mind; soul.

NESHAMA: the soul.

NOACHIDE LAWS: the seven basic Divine commandments incumbent upon non-Jews.

'OLAM HA-BA: the World to Come.

'OLAM HA-ZEH: this world.

'OMER: (1) the seven-week period from the second day of PESAH to SHAVUOT; (2) a sheaf of wheat brought as a sacrifice.

'ONEG SHABBAT: pleasure and delight in the Sabbath.

OSHER: happiness.

'OSHER: riches.

PARASHA: portion of the Torah.

PARSHAT...: the weekly Torah-reading called...

PARSHIYOT: sections of the Torah contained in the *tefillin*.

PESAH: Passover.

PETIRAH: death.

PIRKEY AVOT: *Ethics of the Fathers*, a MISHNA tractate.

PIYYUT (PIYYUTIM): a liturgical poem.

RABBENU: our teacher.

RAMBAM: Maimonides.

RAMBAN: Nachmanides.

RASHA' (RESHA'IM): a wicked person.

RAV: a rabbi; a teacher.

ROSH HASHANA: the Jewish New Year; the first day of TISHREI.

RUAH: spirit; soul.

SEFIRAH: singular of SEFIROT.

SEFIROT: the ten mystical spheres or levels described in KABBALA.

SELIHOT: special penitential prayers.

SHABBAT (SHABBATOT): the Sabbath.

SHAVUOT: Pentecost.

SHECHINA: the Divine Presence.

SHELO LISHMAH: not for its own sake; for ulterior motives.

SHEMA': "Hear O Israel..." (*Devarim* 6:5), the opening words of the fundamental Jewish prayer which proclaims the unity of God.

SHEMINI ATZERET: the eighth day of SUKKOT.

SHEMONEH 'ESREH: the Eighteen Benedictions, or *'Amida* prayer.

SHEMOT: the Book of Exodus.

SHE'OL: Hell.

SHIR HA-MA'ALOT: "Song of Degrees."

SHIR HA-SHIRIM: the Song of Songs.

SHIUR: a lesson; a lecture.

SHLOMO HA-MELECH: King Solomon.

SHOFTIM: Judges.

SHOHET: a Jewish ritual slaughterer.

SIMHAT TORAH: holiday of rejoicing in the giving of the Torah.

SUKKA: a temporary structure lived in during the holiday of SUKKOT.

SUKKOT: the Festival of Tabernacles.

TALMID (TALMIDIM): a student; a disciple.

TALMID HACHAM (TALMIDEI HACHAMIM): a person learned in the Torah.

TANACH: the Bible, comprising the Humash (Pentateuch), the Prophets and the Writings.

TANNA (TANNAIM): the Sage(s) whose traditions and opinions comprise the MISHNA.

TANYA: the seminal work of Habad Hassidut.

TARGUM: the Aramaic version of the Bible.

TEHOM: the primeval waters; the waters below the earth.

TERAFIM: objects used for divination (*Bereshit* 31:19,30).

TERUMA: obligatory offerings to KOHANIM.

TESHUVA: repentance.

TIKKUN: self-improvement; rectification.

TIRHA DE-TSIBBURA: (A.) an imposition on the public.

TISHREI: the month which begins the Jewish year.

TSADDEKET: a righteous woman.

TSADDIK (TSADDIKIM): a righteous man.

TSARA'AT: leprosy.

TSIMMES: (Y.) a sweetened vegetable side dish.

TSITSIT: fringes.

TUM'AH: ritual impurity.

URIM AND TUMMIM: means for receiving communications from God (*Shemot* 28:30).

YALKUT (SHIMONI): a Midrashic compendium.

YAMIM HA-NORAIM: the "Days of Awe"; the High Holy Days.

YEREI SHAMAYIM: a God-fearing person.
YERUSHALMI : the Jerusalem Talmud.
YESHIVA: an academy of Torah study.
YETZER: inclination (usually referring to YETZER HA-RA').
YETZER HA-RA': the evil inclination.
YETZER HA-TOV: the good inclination.
YIR'AT SHAMAYIM: fear of Heaven.
YOM KIPPUR: the Day of Atonement, which falls on the
  10th day of TISHREI.
YOM TOV: a festival.

ZATSAL: an acronym which means "may his memory be a
  blessing"; (abbr. z.ts.l.)
ZECHUT (ZECHUYOT): merit.